Zero-Proof Celebrations

The Holiday Host's Guide to Festive Alcohol-Free Drinks

and Gatherings

Nicci Brochard
&
Dr. Ben Chuba

Zero-Proof Celebrations

The Holiday Host's Guide to Festive Alcohol-Free Drinks

and Gatherings

Book Formatting by: Monisha

Book cover design by: *Billy Design*

CROSSBORDER

New York, London, Quebec

Contents

Introduction

The clinking of glasses, the warmth of shared laughter, and the sparkle of celebration; these moments define our most cherished gatherings. Yet for too long, the assumption has persisted that memorable parties require alcohol to fuel the festivities. This misconception has left countless hosts scrambling to accommodate guests who don't drink, often relegating them to bland sodas or plain water while everyone else enjoys thoughtfully crafted beverages.

The landscape of entertaining is shifting dramatically. Millions of people are choosing sobriety, reducing their alcohol intake, or simply preferring alternatives that allow them to remain fully present during special moments. Pregnant guests, designated drivers, those taking medications, and individuals who simply enjoy clear-headed celebrations deserve the same attention to detail and creativity that traditional cocktails receive.

Zero-proof entertaining represents far more than substitution; it embodies innovation, inclusivity, and intentionality. The art lies in understanding how flavors dance together, how presentation elevates experience, and how thoughtful preparation transforms simple ingredients into memorable moments. Sophisticated mocktails can rival any traditional cocktail in complexity and visual appeal, while alcohol-free punches and seasonal specialties create focal points that bring people together.

This guide will transform your approach to hosting, providing you with the knowledge and confidence to create celebrations where every guest feels valued and included. You'll discover flavor profiles that surprise and delight, presentation techniques that photograph beautifully, and menu planning strategies that ensure seamless execution.

The most meaningful celebrations happen when barriers dissolve and connections flourish. By mastering the art of zero-proof entertaining, you're not limiting your hosting abilities, you're expanding them. You're creating space for authentic conversations, genuine laughter, and memories that guests will treasure long after the last glass is cleared. The future of festive gatherings is bright, inclusive, and deliciously alcohol-free.

Nicci and I (Ben) thank you immensely for choosing our book. Cheers to the party ahead.

Chapter 1

Cheers to Change – The Zero-Proof Holiday Movement

The clink of glasses and cries of "cheers!" are familiar sounds at any holiday gathering. But listen closely at celebrations these days and you might notice something different: more glasses filled with sparkling cider, artisanal mocktails, or alcohol-free bubbly. A powerful cultural shift is underway in how we celebrate. Welcome to the zero-proof holiday movement – a new era where *everyone* can raise a glass. This movement isn't about dampening fun or judging those who imbibe; it's about choice, inclusivity, and wellness. In this chapter, we'll explore how the "sober curious" trend is transforming holiday socializing, how younger generations are reviving the art of the dinner party (with creative twists and without the hangovers), the surging demand for booze-free options, and the warm, mindful approach to festivities that ensures no guest feels left out. By the end, you'll see why alcohol-free entertaining is quickly becoming the heart of modern holiday celebrations.

The Sober-Curious Shift

Not long ago, offering a non-alcoholic option at a holiday party meant maybe a soda or a bit of lemon water in the corner. Today, that token gesture has evolved into a full-fledged movement. The "sober curious" shift refers to a growing number of people who are actively rethinking their relationship with alcohol – especially during social events. This trend isn't about declaring lifelong teetotaling or sucking all the merriment out of parties. Instead, it's a wellness-driven exploration of drinking habits. Many folks are choosing to cut back or take breaks from alcohol, and they're discovering that celebrations can be just as fun (if not more so) without the booze. In fact, industry observers note that a powerful "sober curious" wave is *"driving a boom in the market for sophisticated alcohol-free alternatives"* as people cut back on traditional alcoholic beverages. Rather than being an afterthought, zero-proof drinks are becoming centerpieces of holiday gatherings.

So, what's fueling this sober-curious surge? A big part of it is a collective focus on health and mindfulness. Consumers are increasingly wellness-minded, paying attention to what they put in their bodies – and that extends to drinks. Alcohol, with its empty calories and next-day headaches, is no longer the automatic life-of-the-party it once was. People have become mindful of the effects of heavy drinking on their sleep, mood, and overall well-being. We've all heard of *Dry January* (taking the month off from alcohol after the New Year) which has opened many eyes to how good one can feel without the nightly glass of wine. It turns out you don't need alcohol to unwind or celebrate – and a lot of us are waking up to that fact. The sober-curious approach encourages pausing and questioning: "Do I really want that drink, or am I just having it out of habit?" Often, simply asking the question leads partygoers to try a tasty alcohol-free alternative instead.

Another driver of this shift comes from generational change. Younger adults, in particular, are drinking less than their predecessors. Some of this is a legal thing (18-20 year-olds often can't drink yet), but even those of legal age in Gen Z consume less alcohol than previous generations did at the same age. Surveys have found that a remarkably high share of young adults – in one case, 42% of those aged 18–24 – report that they *never* drink alcohol, far above the average for all adults. That's a sea change in social behavior. These younger folks aren't necessarily swearing off fun; they're just finding that fun in other ways. For many Gen Z and Millennial revelers, skipping the beer or spiked punch is about feeling good *during* the party and *after* it. They've seen older generations battle hangovers or health issues and are consciously choosing a different path.

Crucially, the beverage industry has noticed this change and responded in style. Gone are the days when a "mocktail" meant a syrupy sweet Shirley Temple that only the non-drinker in the room would reluctantly sip. Now we have a booming market of alcohol-free beers, wines, and spirits that are crafted with as much care as the real thing. Think rich, hoppy non-alcoholic IPAs, or distilled botanical "spirits" that mimic gin and whiskey using herbs and spices – minus the alcohol. There are sparkling celebratory drinks, elegant bottles and packaging, and flavor profiles so sophisticated you forget there's no liquor involved. The shift toward mindful drinking has spurred innovation: one market analysis forecasts an 18.5% average annual growth in sales of non-alcoholic beer, cocktails, spirits, and wine alternatives through 2029. In other words, the zero-proof cocktail is not a passing fad – it's a formidable new segment that's here to stay.

All of this means that holiday socializing is undergoing a healthy makeover. The "cheers to change" isn't just a cute phrase – it's literal. At holiday dinners, you might see a table where the champagne flutes are filled with alcohol-free bubbly tinged with elderflower and pear. At New Year's Eve parties, more guests are welcoming midnight with a glass of sparkling cider or a craft mocktail in hand. No one's feeling like they're missing out, because these zero-proof drinks are *fun*. They're often delicious, Instagram-pretty, and come without the worry of overindulgence. The sober-curious movement has made it absolutely clear: a great party doesn't depend on alcohol. You can laugh, dance, clink glasses, and make amazing memories – and still wake up fresh as a daisy the next morning. This new mindset is transforming holiday gatherings everywhere, setting the stage for celebrations that prioritize feeling good both in the moment and the day after.

Millennials & Gen Z: Dinner Party Revival

If you want to see where the zero-proof holiday movement really shines, look no further than the homes of Millennials and Gen Zers. These younger generations are spearheading a dinner party revival – bringing back the art of at-home entertaining, but with modern twists that reflect their values (including a preference for low- or no-alcohol fun). Why is the dinner party making such a comeback? For one, going out to bars and restaurants has gotten *pricey*. A fancy cocktail at a trendy bar can cost as much as an entrée these days, and with many young adults watching their budgets, hosting at home just makes sense. But it's not only about thrift; it's also about control and creativity. When you host your own gathering, you get to set the vibe, curate the guest list, and crucially – decide what's in the punch bowl.

In fact, many Millennials and Gen Z have "soured on drinking" in the bar scene altogether. Instead of meeting up for rounds of drinks downtown, they're more likely to throw a themed potluck, a game night, or a cozy Friendsgiving dinner where everyone brings a dish *and* their favorite alcohol-free beverage to share. Friendsgiving – that modern tradition of celebrating Thanksgiving with friends, often before or in place of family Thanksgiving – has become hugely popular (about 4 in 10 young Americans now celebrate it in some form). At these gatherings, it's not unusual for the host to whip up a signature mocktail as the evening's highlight: maybe a spiced cranberry spritzer with rosemary garnish, or a non-alcoholic hot toddy steaming with cinnamon and cloves. The emphasis is on the experience – great food, great conversation, photogenic drinks – rather than on getting drunk. As a result, the parties feel fresh and inclusive. Guests might actually remember every detail the next day, and nobody has to call a rideshare service at midnight feeling woozy!

It helps that Millennials and Gen Z are a social media-savvy bunch. They love to share the cool things they're doing – and hosting an elegant alcohol-free holiday party is definitely cool. Peek at Instagram or TikTok around the holidays, and you'll find content creators showing off "sober chic" gatherings: a beautiful dinner table set with twinkling lights and garnished mocktails, or a step-by-step video of how to create a Christmas punch that "just happens to be booze-free." The younger generations have essentially *rebranded* the notion of a dry party. No longer is an alcohol-free gathering seen as dull. On the contrary, it's often portrayed as trendy and enlightened. A host might say, "I want my party to be memorable for the conversation and connection, not for anyone drinking too much." In an era when personal wellness is a badge of honor, serving craft kombucha or a non-alcoholic sparkling rosé can be as much of a status symbol as popping a fancy champagne bottle was in the past.

Let's picture a scene to see how Millennials and Gen Z are redefining the holiday house party: It's December, and a group of friends in their twenties and thirties gather for an Ugly Sweater Holiday Party at someone's apartment. The place is decked out in string lights and fun decor. On the kitchen counter, instead of a typical bar laden with liquor bottles, there's a DIY mocktail bar. There are recipe cards for drinks with playful names like "Winter Wonderland Spritz" (made with alcohol-free gin, tonic, and peppermint syrup) and "Cranberry Kiss" (a bubbly concoction of cranberry juice, ginger beer, and lime). There's bowls of fresh garnishes – cranberries, orange slices, mint, candied ginger – so guests can personalize their drinks. As people arrive, they're actually excited to try these creations. One guest snaps a photo of their vibrant red mocktail against the backdrop of holiday lights and posts it with a hashtag like #ZeroProofParty. Laughter fills the air, holiday music is playing, and everyone is fully engaged in conversation or a spirited game of "White Elephant" gift exchange. What's notably absent is anyone getting sloppy. By the end of the night, the consensus is that this was one of the best parties of the season, and nobody has to nurse a hangover tomorrow. This scenario isn't a wishful fantasy – it's happening more and more in real life as young adults redefine how to party.

Economic and cultural forces both play a role here. As mentioned, the cost of a night out in the city can be prohibitive – why spend $15 on a single cocktail when you can buy an entire bottle of gourmet alcohol-free mixer for the same price and serve all your friends? Moreover, the pandemic years taught a lot of people how cozy and fulfilling home gatherings can be. Millennials and Gen Z picked up cooking, baking, and *mixology* (or shall we say "mocktail-ology") skills while stuck at home, and now they're eager to showcase those talents. There's a sense of occasion to hosting a dinner party – it feels grown-up and intimate. Younger hosts have discovered that by cutting alcohol out of the equation or minimizing it, the focus shifts to *other* creative elements: themed menus, elaborate dessert boards, or interactive activities like cocktail-making competitions – with zero-proof recipes, of course. And guess what? Nobody misses the booze. The fun, the flavor, and the friendship are more than enough.

Importantly, this shift doesn't mean younger generations never drink or that every gathering is dry. It means they're intentional about when and how they include alcohol. Many are choosing to drink less frequently, and when they do host boozy beverages, they do so alongside equally enticing non-alcoholic ones. At a Friendsgiving, for example, you might find a spiked apple cider on the stove *and* a non-alcoholic mulled cider right next to it, so each guest can choose. The key is that the zero-proof option is given equal billing – it's not the sad little sibling to the "real" drink. Often, the alcohol-free version ends up just as popular, if not more so, because even people who usually drink might switch over to keep sharp for the drive home or simply to avoid feeling groggy. In this way, Millennials and Gen Z hosts are normalizing mindful drinking. It's simply part of the new dinner party code: provide great food, great entertainment, and great drinks *for everyone* – and that means plenty of creative non-alcoholic choices.

Surging Demand for Booze-Free Options

The rise of zero-proof celebrations isn't just anecdotal – it's visible in hard numbers and industry feedback. Over the past few holiday seasons, there has been an explosion in demand for booze-free drink options at events big and small. Ask any forward-thinking event planner or caterer, and they'll tell you the same thing: if you're not offering non-alcoholic drinks, you're behind the times. One event catering company's beverage director even reported, *"We've seen requests for non-alcoholic options increase by nearly 60% for New Year's Eve events in the past two years,"* reflecting a broad move toward mindful drinking during the holidays. That kind of spike is eye-opening – it means that more than ever, people ringing in the New Year want celebratory drinks *without* the alcohol. It's not because parties have become tame; it's because hosts and guests alike are realizing you can have all the festive fizz and flavor without the booze. The trend is clear: mocktails and low-ABV drinks are taking their place alongside champagne and eggnog on the holiday menu.

This surging demand is reshaping how venues and hosts prepare for gatherings. Just a few years ago, a typical holiday party at a banquet hall might have had one token "mocktail" on request or a couple of bottles of sparkling grape juice for the non-drinkers. Now, we're seeing full-fledged zero-proof cocktail bars set up at events. For instance, at a corporate New Year's gala, the organizers might hire mixologists who specialize in alcohol-free cocktails to shake up drinks all night – everything from virgin mojitos with fresh mint to complex mocktail martinis with botanical infusions. Wedding planners have noted similar shifts for winter weddings and holiday-themed events: the couple might insist on a rich menu of non-alcoholic beers and wines, so that guests who aren't drinking have just as many gourmet choices as those who are. In fact, some bars and restaurants host "Zero-Proof Nights" or include robust alcohol-free sections on their drink menus year-round now. The movement during the holidays is part of a larger hospitality industry response where no- and low-alcohol beverages are one of the fastest-growing segments. According to one consumer insights report, share of the non-alcoholic beverages category in late 2023 jumped 62% compared to the year prior – and over 100% since 2021. Those numbers underline just how rapidly the landscape is changing; venues are practically scrambling to keep up with the thirst for inventive booze-free beverages.

What's driving this surge, besides consumer wellness trends? One factor is simply that the options available are far better than they used to be. When you give people delicious choices, they'll take them. Craft brewers have perfected non-alcoholic beers that taste almost indistinguishable from regular brews – hoppy, bold, and satisfying. Winemakers have developed dealcoholized wines that still bring complexity and aroma to the glass (no more super-sweet sparkling grape juice that tastes like kiddie stuff). And the spirits world has seen an influx of distilled botanicals: for example, alcohol-free aperitifs made from herbs and fruit that have a bitter, sophisticated bite to mimic Campari or gin alternatives that deliver the juniper and spice notes gin-lovers expect. With such quality on the market, hosts can offer a serious adult beverage experience without the alcohol content. Guests aren't just saying "I guess I'll have water since I'm driving"; instead, they're saying "Ooh, I'll have the smoked coconut margarita mocktail, please!" and genuinely looking forward to it.

Another driver is the inclusive mindset hosts are embracing. Party-givers have always wanted their guests to enjoy themselves – that's nothing new. What *is* new is the awareness that a significant chunk of any guest list might appreciate non-alcoholic options. Perhaps Grandma doesn't drink for health reasons, your friend is expecting a baby, your coworker is on medication that doesn't mix with alcohol, or someone simply doesn't like the taste of booze. In the past, those folks were often overlooked, left with a lonely can of club soda. Now, hosts are actively planning to delight *all* their guests. They're stocking up on fancy NA beverages and even learning mixology tricks to make sure the presentation is top-notch. The result? Events where nobody feels like an afterthought. It's common now to see a beautifully arranged "mocktail station" at a holiday open house, right next to the regular bar. Picture a table draped in festive cloth, twinkling with string lights, where colorful alcohol-free drinks are pre-mixed in pretty pitchers or can be custom-made. A chalkboard sign might read "Zero-Proof Specials: Pomegranate Ginger Punch & Holiday Nojito (mint, lime, soda)." Guests flock to it out of curiosity, and many end up trying both the alcoholic and non-alcoholic offerings throughout the night. This kind of setup acknowledges that *everyone* deserves something special in their glass when it's time for a toast.

We should also note that this demand surge has a feedback loop: the more people request booze-free options, the more the industry creates, and the better those options get – which in turn attracts even more people to try them. It's a virtuous cycle. Event caterers have observed that once a host includes a few non-alcoholic cocktails on the menu, those drinks often run out *just as quickly* as the alcoholic ones. That's a strong sign that even guests who normally drink alcohol are partaking in – and enjoying – the zero-proof choices. Part of it is curiosity ("Hmm, what does a gin-free gin and tonic taste like?") and part is practicality ("I've had one spiked cocktail, so I'll switch to mocktails for the rest of the night so I can drive home safely."). The bottom line is that mindful drinking – the practice of being deliberate about if and how much one drinks – is on full display during the holidays. People want to celebrate without overdoing it, and providing great zero-proof drinks is the perfect solution. It keeps the spirit high and the risk low. As hosts catch on to this trend, they're proactively planning their parties with an eye toward these offerings, ensuring they don't run dry of alcohol-free bubbly by 10 PM. From the standpoint of venues and caterers, adapting to this wave isn't just good manners – it's good business. After all, when nearly half the crowd is asking for mocktails, you'd better have the supply (and creative recipes) to meet the demand!

Inclusive & Mindful Festivities

Ultimately, the zero-proof holiday movement is about inclusion and mindful celebration. The ethos here is simple: everyone deserves to be part of the party. For too many years, non-drinkers found themselves on the sidelines of holiday festivities, often with nothing festive in their hand to sip. As one sober lifestyle blogger quipped, *"We've spent too many years sipping on lemon water or coffee at holiday gatherings."* That quote might draw a chuckle, but it speaks to a real gap in traditional entertaining – a gap this book is eager to help close. No one should feel left out just because they're not drinking alcohol, whether it's by choice, for health, or any other reason. Inclusive festivities mean that when the host raises a toast, *every* guest can raise a gorgeous glass of something sparkly, tasty, and celebratory. The clink of glasses should ring all around, not just from those holding champagne flutes. As one expert rightly noted, holiday traditions like parties and toasts *"shouldn't just be reserved for those drinking alcohol."* There's a certain joy and camaraderie in toasting together, and that moment belongs to everyone at the table.

Embracing zero-proof options is also about hosting more mindfully. What does mindful hosting look like? It means thinking about your guests' comfort and enjoyment in a holistic way. A mindful host will consider things like: Will my guests be able to drive home safely? Will they feel good tomorrow? Is anyone on a diet or medication that means they want to avoid alcohol tonight? By planning a party that offers plenty of non-alcoholic delights, the host is essentially saying, *"I see you, I value you, and I want you to have an equally fantastic time."* It removes any stigma from not drinking. In a mindful, inclusive gathering, a guest can freely decline alcohol without feeling awkward or pressured, because there are appealing alternatives right there. The social dynamic shifts too – it becomes perfectly normal for someone to be happily sipping a zero-proof cocktail, and nobody bats an eye or teases them with "Oh, come on, live a little!" The truth is, they *are* living a lot – fully present and engaged in the celebration.

Another beautiful aspect of inclusive, alcohol-free (or alcohol-optional) festivities is the quality of connection that often results. When people aren't over-imbibing, conversations can be deeper and more memorable. Grandma can tell her favorite childhood holiday story and everyone is truly listening, not tuning out after their third glass of wine. The kids at the gathering – if it's a family party – see that the adults can have fun without beer bottles in hand, which sends a positive message. Even those who do choose to drink at an inclusive party tend to do so more moderately, because the vibe encourages balance. It's a ripple effect of mindfulness. For example, at a workplace holiday party that prominently features an enticing zero-proof cocktail menu, employees who might have felt obligated to drink (to fit in or network) can relax and enjoy a "mocktail mule" or a virgin piña colada without any loss of social capital. In fact, it can become a conversation piece: *"Have you tried the pomegranate punch? It's amazing – can you believe it has no alcohol?"* When the focus is on flavors and festivities rather than the buzz, people often mingle more freely and remember the night more clearly. That leads to warm memories instead of "ugh, what did I say to my boss after that third cocktail…?" the next day.

The shift to inclusive hosting is also sparking creativity and joy in hosts. Freed from the default of "beer, wine, and a signature alcoholic punch," hosts are experimenting with all sorts of new recipes and ideas. They're finding inspiration in seasonal ingredients – cranberries, peppermint, apple cider, nutmeg – to craft drinks that feel holiday-specific and special. Some hosts set up interactive drink-making stations, where guests can mix their own mocktails, choosing from a variety of juices, flavored syrups, fresh fruits, and herbs. It becomes an activity in itself, much like decorating cookies or gingerbread houses. Others curate a tasting of store-bought non-alcoholic beverages, effectively creating a little NA bar. You might see a host put out several brands of alcohol-free beers or sparkling wines and encourage guests to give feedback like a mini tasting event ("The raspberry sparkling wine is delicious, but try the white one – it's got a lovely crisp finish!"). These kinds of touches make the non-drinking guests feel not just accommodated, but celebrated. The inclusion isn't begrudging; it's enthusiastic.

Perhaps the most heartwarming outcome of all this is how it allows *everyone* to fully participate in the holiday magic. When midnight strikes on New Year's Eve, you don't have one segment of people cheering with champagne and another hovering quietly in the background – instead, every glass is raised. The toast is truly shared by all. And the next morning, the group chat is buzzing not with complaints of hangovers, but with photos from the night, recipes for that amazing gingerbread mocktail, and plans to do it all again soon. By crafting gatherings where alcohol is an option rather than the default star of the show, we ensure that every guest goes home with only good memories. No one has to miss work the next day due to over-celebrating, and nobody at the party felt like the odd one out. In a very real sense, zero-proof gatherings make the holidays *more* joyous – they strip away some potential negatives (like hangovers, conflict, or exclusion) and amplify the positives (laughter, connection, taste, and inclusivity).

As we raise our glasses to this new era of holiday hosting, remember that the goal isn't to banish alcohol entirely or judge anyone's choices. It's about expanding the possibilities of celebration. A zero-proof party simply means that whether someone is abstaining for the night or for life, they get to partake in the full experience. With the ideas and insights in this guide, you'll be able to elevate every toast, craft every cocktail (or "mocktail"), and create a celebratory atmosphere where no one feels left out. The holidays are about coming together in warmth and friendship – and there's no requirement that a bottle of booze be on the table to achieve that. By embracing the zero-proof movement, you're tapping into a trend that's modern, thoughtful, and truly in the spirit of the season. So cheers to change, and cheers to inclusive, hangover-free celebrations that everyone can enjoy. The party has only just begun, and it's already shaping up to be one for the ages – with memories that all will cherish, clear-headed and happy.

Chapter 2

Mixology Minus the Alcohol – Building Your Zero-Proof Bar

Welcome to the heart of your zero-proof journey: building a bar that's completely alcohol-free yet fully equipped for festive mixology. In this chapter, we'll walk through how to stock your zero-proof bar with all the essentials and extras that make for truly special drinks. Just because you're skipping the booze doesn't mean you're skimping on flavor or sophistication. In fact, crafting alcohol-free cocktails (a.k.a. mocktails) uses the same mixology fundamentals as any great cocktail – you'll be measuring, shaking, stirring, and always asking yourself the key question every good bartender does: "Is it delicious?". With a warm and adventurous spirit, let's dive into the ingredients, tools, techniques, and finishing touches that will make your zero-proof bar the envy of any holiday host.

Stocking Your Zero-Proof Bar

The first step to mixology minus the alcohol is stocking your bar with flavorful, high-quality ingredients. Approach it just like stocking a traditional bar – only the bottles are different. A well-stocked zero-proof bar ensures you can create an array of drinks to suit every taste, from sweet and fruity to spicy and bitter. Here's a practical guide to the must-haves:

- **Fresh Pressed Juices & Flavorful Bases:** Juices are the backbone of many alcohol-free cocktails, providing natural sweetness, color, and body. Freshly squeezed citrus juices (like lemon, lime, and orange) are essential for sours, spritzes, and punches. Have some apple cider or cranberry juice for seasonal warmth, and perhaps pineapple or grapefruit juice for tropical vibes. Don't overlook vegetable juices or unique bases like carrot, beet, or cucumber juice for creative twists – they add earthiness and vibrant color. For convenience, you can stock high-quality cold-pressed juices from the store, but whenever possible, fresh is best (a quick squeeze of a lemon right before mixing can elevate a drink's brightness). If you really want to get fancy, consider making or buying herbal infusions and teas as bases: for example, brew strong hibiscus tea for a tart red mocktail base, or steep chamomile, mint, or green tea to use as interesting mixers. These herbal infusions bring nuanced flavors and aromas that plain juice or soda might not, layering in complexity without any alcohol.

- **Non-Alcoholic Spirits (Zero-Proof Liquors):** One of the secrets to creating mocktails with the depth and complexity of cocktails is using the new wave of non-alcoholic distilled spirits. These products are specifically crafted to mimic the flavors and even the mouthfeel of spirits like gin, whiskey, tequila, rum, and aperitifs – so your mocktails can have the same nuanced character as their boozy counterparts. For example, you can find gin alternatives distilled with juniper and botanicals, whiskey alternatives with oak, vanilla, and smoke notes, and aperitif alternatives brimming with bitter herbs and citrus. Stocking a few of these bottles will open up a world of possibilities. *What exactly are these magical spirits?* They go by various names – spirit alternatives, elixirs, botanicals – but essentially they're alcohol-free liquors. Some are made by traditional distillation with the alcohol removed, and others by blending botanicals, extracts, and spices to simulate the aroma and "kick" of booze. A great one to start with is Seedlip, the pioneering brand that created a gin-like herbal spirit without any fermentation or alcohol (their bottle is *beautiful* and the liquid has a lovely garden-fresh taste). Many hosts also swear by Ritual Zero Proof (they make excellent gin, whiskey, rum, and tequila alternatives that win points for realism) and Lyre's, an Australian brand offering a whole portfolio of spirit stand-ins – from a Dry London Spirit (gin alternative) to American Malt (whiskey) and even an Italian Spritz that emulates a classic aperitivo. If you're a whiskey cocktail fan, you might try Spiritless Kentucky 74, a non-alcoholic bourbon that's actually born from real bourbon – the makers distill a full-strength whiskey then remove the alcohol, leaving behind those oaky, caramel flavors and even a hint of heat to mimic the "burn". For gin lovers, Monday Gin is often praised for its juniper-forward authenticity, while Free Spirits makes a terrific tequila alternative (their "Spirit of Tequila" has the smoky-agave bite tequila drinkers crave. You don't need dozens of bottles; just pick a few favorites that match the cocktails you love. For instance, if you adore margaritas or palomas, grab a tequila alternative; if you're into martinis and G&Ts, a gin alternative is key; if you fancy cozy whiskey sours or Old Fashioneds, get a whiskey alternative. These bottles will be the backbone of reinventing classic drinks without the booze.

- **Quality Mixers (Sodas, Sparkling and More):** In any bar, mixers are the supporting cast that can make a good drink great. In a zero-proof bar, they're just as crucial. Stock up on premium sodas and sparkling waters – think tonic water, club soda, and ginger beer. Quality matters here: a craft tonic (like Fever-Tree or Q Mixers) brings quinine bitterness and fine bubbles that can elevate a simple mocktail into something classy. Ginger beer (spicy and robust, usually non-alcoholic despite the name) is fantastic for adding a kick to drinks (hello, virgin Moscow Mules and Dark & Stormies). Don't forget ginger ale, cola, or lemonade as additional mixers for certain recipes. And if you're feeling adventurous, consider having some fermented mixers: kombucha (fermented tea) or water kefir can act as a tangy, funky sparkling base that provides a complexity similar to beer or cider. Even a non-alcoholic beer or dealcoholized wine can be used creatively in cocktails, though those might shine more in Chapter 3 when we entertain different drink options. The idea is to have a variety of carbonation and flavor on hand – something spicy, something bitter, something sweet, something dry – so you can top off or lengthen any mocktail with just the right fizz or flavor.

- **Syrups and Sweeteners:** A well-stocked zero-proof bar also needs a few syrups. Classic simple syrup (sugar dissolved in water) is a must for balancing tart ingredients, and you can easily make it at home and keep a jar in the fridge. Beyond that, explore flavored syrups: vanilla syrup, caramel, honey syrup, agave nectar, maple syrup, or fruit syrups like grenadine (pomegranate syrup) and orgeat (almond syrup) can add depth and sweetness. Many classic cocktail recipes rely on a hint of sweetness for balance, and your mocktails will too. You can purchase high-quality syrups (Monin, Liber & Co., and Torani are popular brands), or make your own infusions by simmering sugar with things like ginger, rosemary, or berries to create custom flavors. Another tip: herbal and spiced syrups are a zero-proof mixologist's best friend. For example, a ginger-lime syrup can bring a zesty punch, a cinnamon-clove syrup can add holiday spice, or a rosemary-thyme syrup can lend an aromatic, sophisticated note to a drink. By stocking a range of sweeteners, you ensure you can adjust the sweet-sour balance of any drink and also layer on flavor (syrups don't just sweeten; they carry the essence of whatever you infused in them).

- **Bitters and Flavor Extracts:** Now, let's talk about the secret weapon that turns "just juice" into a cocktail-like concoction: bitters. Bitters are essentially highly concentrated flavor extracts made from herbs, spices, and bitter botanicals – they were traditionally made with alcohol, but are used only by the drop or dash. The good news for zero-proof hosts is that many bitters are either alcohol-free or have alcohol-free alternatives available. There are now bitters brands that use glycerin or other means to extract flavors without alcohol (for example, the brand All The Bitter offers a fantastic alcohol-free bitters trio with classic flavors like aromatic and orange). Even traditional bitters like Angostura or Peychaud's, though technically made with alcohol, contribute such minuscule amounts per dash that some people choose to include them in mocktails – that's a personal choice. Either way, do include bitters in your bar stock. Just a few drops of aromatic bitters can completely transform a drink – bringing in notes of clove, cinnamon, gentian root, citrus peel, or whatever blend of spices used. Think of bitters as the spice rack of your bar: those little bottles of magic are like salt and pepper for drinks, adding layers of flavor and complexity with just a dash or two. In addition to cocktail bitters, consider other extracts and flavor boosters: a splash of vanilla extract or almond extract can deepen flavor (make sure they're alcohol-free, or again used sparingly), and flower waters like rosewater or orange blossom water can add an elegant aromatic twist. By stocking a variety of bitters and extracts, you ensure your mocktails won't taste one-note – you'll have the means to season and deepen flavors just as a mixologist would with alcoholic liqueurs or bitters.

- **Fresh Produce and Spices:** Last but certainly not least, remember to have fresh fruits, herbs, and spices on hand. These are the building blocks of garnishes and also often ingredients in the drink. Keep a selection of citrus fruits (lemons, limes, oranges, grapefruit) in your kitchen – their juice is key and their peels make great twists or zests for aroma. Have some fresh berries or seasonal fruits for muddling into drinks or garnishing on picks. Stock up on herbs like mint, basil, rosemary, and thyme; a slap of fresh mint or a sprig of rosemary can wake up a mocktail with bright aroma and color. Spices such as cinnamon sticks, whole star anise, cloves, nutmeg, or even chili peppers can be used to infuse syrups, garnish glasses, or float in a punch bowl for flavor. Ginger root is another all-star – you can muddle fresh ginger or juice it for spicy heat, or use candied ginger as a garnish. Having a little assortment of these perishable but important items whenever you're hosting ensures that your zero-proof drinks will be bursting with freshness and sensory appeal. Remember, you can't stock these indefinitely, but plan to buy fresh ingredients before your gathering. Think of it this way: your zero-proof bar isn't just the bottles on the shelf, but also the contents of your fridge and pantry. A truly well-stocked bar has both the shelf-stable mixers and bottles *and* the fresh elements that bring a drink to life.

By thoughtfully stocking your zero-proof bar with the ingredients above, you set yourself up for success. You'll be able to follow virtually any mocktail recipe – or invent your own – because you'll have the essential building blocks for flavor at your fingertips. From here, we move on to the fun part: using those tools and techniques to mix up fantastic drinks.

Tools and Techniques

Stocking great ingredients is half the battle; now you need to know how to mix them like a pro. The good news is that making a great mocktail isn't so different from making a cocktail. You'll be using many of the same bartending tools and techniques – just without the liquor. This section gives an overview of the key tools every zero-proof host should have, and some tips on technique to craft drinks with professional flair.

Essential Bar Tools: Even in a zero-proof bar, you'll want the classic bartending tools on hand. The basics include a shaker, a muddler, a jigger, a bar spoon, and a strainer. If those sound fancy, don't worry – you might already have some in your kitchen, or you can easily get an affordable cocktail kit that contains all of them. A cocktail shaker (either a two-piece Boston shaker or a three-piece cobbler shaker with a built-in strainer) is used for shaking drinks with ice. This is important for cocktails (and mocktails) that contain juices, syrups, or thicker ingredients – shaking vigorously with ice chills the drink and gives it a nice dilution for balance. A muddler is a baton-like tool used to mash or "muddle" ingredients – for instance, crushing mint leaves to release their oils for a mojito, or smashing berries or citrus in the bottom of a glass to extract flavor. A jigger is simply a small double-sided measuring cup, typically with one side measuring 1 ounce and the other 2 ounces (or other common increments). Using a jigger to measure your ingredients ensures consistency and balance – mixology is part art, part science, and good measurement can make the difference between a drink that's perfectly balanced and one that's too strong (or in the case of mocktails, perhaps too sweet or too sour). A long bar spoon is used for stirring drinks (usually those made only with clear ingredients, like spirit alternatives plus purely liquid modifiers) and for layering liquids if needed. And a strainer (like a Hawthorne strainer that fits in a shaker tin, or a fine mesh strainer for extra clarity) helps you pour a drink from the shaker without ice or muddled bits of fruit plopping into the glass.

Bonus Tools: Depending on how deep you want to go, there are a few additional tools that can elevate your zero-proof cocktail game. A citrus juicer or reamer is incredibly handy for extracting fresh lemon/lime juice quickly. A blender is great for frozen mocktails or blending fruit-based drinks to a smooth consistency (frozen virgin margaritas or piña coladas, anyone?). A mixing glass (a heavy glass pitcher) can be useful for stirring drinks that need chilling without shaking. And don't forget basic things like a cutting board and a sharp knife for prepping fruit and garnishes. If you really want to show off, you could even get an electric frother or whisk for whipping up foams or mixing egg-white alternatives like aquafaba to give cocktails a lovely foamy head. But none of that is strictly required – a basic set of tools and some common kitchen items will cover almost all your needs.

Shaking, Stirring, and Straining (Techniques): Now that you have the tools, let's talk technique. One principle of mixology to embrace is that when you mix a drink, you're not just combining flavors – you're also controlling temperature and dilution. Cocktails are meant to be served cold and balanced, and the same goes for mocktails. So, if a recipe calls for shaking, don't skip that step thinking "there's no alcohol, so why bother?" Shaking with ice is what chills the drink down and adds the right amount of water to soften intense flavors. Generally, you shake drinks that contain juices, syrups, or thicker ingredients – give a good hard shake for about 10-15 seconds until the shaker is frosty on the outside. This introduces air (adding a pleasant light texture) and ensures a thorough mix. Stirring with ice is the technique for cocktails that are all spirits (or in our case, spirit alternatives) and clear mixers – for example, if you were making a zero-proof version of a martini or Manhattan. Use a bar spoon to gently stir the drink with ice for a longer time (20-30 seconds) to chill without too much aeration, yielding a silky texture. After shaking or stirring, use your strainer to pour the drink into your serving glass, holding back the ice. The result should be cold, crisp, and perfectly diluted – a mocktail that feels as refreshing and expertly made as any cocktail.

A quick note on technique: don't be afraid to taste as you go. Since there's no raw alcohol to worry about, you can sip your concoction from the mixing tin with a straw (or a spoon) before you pour it out. If it's too tart, add a touch more sweetener; if it's too sweet, a squeeze more citrus; if it's flat, maybe a dash more bitters or a splash of soda. This kind of adjustment is exactly what seasoned mixologists do. Remember, you're aiming for a balanced flavor and you have all these tools and ingredients at your disposal to tweak the drink until, yes, it's delicious.

Layering Flavors with Care: Just like with alcoholic cocktails, crafting a great mocktail means layering flavors thoughtfully. You generally start with your base (perhaps a non-alcoholic spirit or a juice), then add your modifiers (like syrups, citrus for sour, other juices or tea for complexity), then your seasonings (bitters, a pinch of salt, etc.), and finally top with a mixer if it's a long drink (like topping with sparkling water or ginger beer). Pay attention to balance: a good drink usually has a harmony of sweet and sour, or sweet and bitter, perhaps with a hint of spice or salt to accentuate. We'll go deeper into flavor balancing in the next section, but as a technique, think of building a drink the way you might build a layered dessert or a savory dish – each component should complement the others. For instance, if you muddle fresh berries (sweet/tart) in a glass, you might add a squeeze of lemon (sour) to brighten them, a rosemary sprig to infuse an herbal note, and top it with a spicy ginger ale to add tingle and tie it all together. If that sounds a bit like a science experiment, fear not – once you start practicing, it becomes an intuitive and fun creative process.

Hospitality and Flair: Part of being a great host is not just making a drink, but *presenting* it with a bit of flair. Use your tools with confidence – a dramatic shake over your shoulder or a graceful stir in a crystal mixing glass can become a performance that delights guests. You can even involve guests in the process: let them smell the bitters bottle, or show them how to clap a mint leaf between your palms before garnishing (it releases the aroma!). These little techniques, while not strictly necessary for the drink's taste, add to the experience of zero-proof cocktails being just as special as any other craft cocktails. As you build your skills, you'll find that the ritual of making the drink – measuring, shaking, garnishing – becomes a pleasure in itself. The takeaway here is that mocktail mixology uses the same care and craft as cocktail mixology. Approach your zero-proof creations with the mindset of a mixologist, and you'll produce drinks that are every bit as exciting. As one expert bartender emphasizes, he approaches his mocktails the same way he does any cocktail, starting every creation by asking "Is it delicious?". If the answer is yes, you're doing it right!

Flavorful Foundations

One concern people sometimes have with mocktails is: *Will it taste like a "kiddie drink" or just a glass of juice?* The truth is, a well-crafted alcohol-free drink can be every bit as complex and "grown-up" as a cocktail, as long as you pay attention to building flavor complexity. This section will teach you how to create flavorful foundations for your drinks so they never taste flat or one-dimensional. The key is balancing sweet, sour, bitter, and spice – the same flavor elements that make cocktails interesting.

Think about your favorite cocktail for a moment. It likely has a balance of sweetness (from a liqueur or sugar), acidity (from citrus or other tart ingredients), bitterness (perhaps from bitters or an amaro), and maybe a touch of heat or spice (some spirits have a burn, or the recipe might include a spicy syrup or ginger). We're going to recreate that balance with zero-proof ingredients. Here's a breakdown of the flavor elements and how to get them:

- **Sweet:** This one's straightforward – most cocktails have some sweetness, and in mocktails you'll often rely on the syrups and juices we mentioned earlier to provide it. Sweetness isn't just about sugar for sugar's sake; it's there to balance sourness or bitterness. The goal is not to make the drink sugary, but to have enough sweetness that, combined with other elements, the flavor is harmonious. You might get sweetness from fruit juices (apple, pineapple, orange all bring natural sugars), from honey or agave in a recipe, or from added syrups like a vanilla syrup in a cream soda-style mocktail, etc. Don't overdo it – start with a little and add more to taste, as it's hard to fix an overly sweet drink except by diluting it.

- **Sour/Tart:** The counterpoint to sweet is sour. This is usually from citrus juice – lemon, lime, grapefruit, etc. A squeeze of lemon or lime can magically brighten a dull drink and cut through sweetness. Other sources of acidity include vinegar-based syrups known as shrubs (for example, a raspberry vinegar shrub can add a fruity tartness and complexity) or even a splash of verjus (a tart, non-alcoholic juice made from unripe grapes, used in fancy bars for acidity). In building your drink, you often start by balancing sweet and sour to get a base that's pleasant – like how lemonade is basically sugar + lemon balanced with water. In a mocktail, once you have that basic sweet-tart balance down, you can layer in the more exotic elements like bitter and spice.

- **Bitter:** Why bitterness in a drink? In cocktails, bitter components (like bitters, or the quinine in tonic, or Campari-like liqueurs) are crucial for depth. Bitterness adds an adult flavor profile – something a kid's drink definitely wouldn't have – and it also slows down the sipping. Think about it: a very sweet lemonade you might gulp down, but a drink with a bitter or complex edge you naturally sip more slowly and savor. One expert mixologist points out that having a bitter or even *hot* component in a mocktail helps duplicate the vibe of a boozy beverage, because alcohol itself has a burn and bitterness that make us pause between sips. "Alcohol and bitter ingredients are two key components to why we can take 10 to 20 minutes or more to drink something that is only 10 to 12 ounces," he notes. To introduce bitterness in your zero-proof drinks, you have a few tools: bitters (discussed above) are the most direct way – a couple dashes of an aromatic bitters or perhaps an orange bitters can do wonders. Another trick is using strongly brewed coffee or tea: a splash of cold brew coffee in a mocktail can lend a subtle bitterness and roasty complexity (great for something like a faux whiskey cola, where a touch of coffee makes it taste darker and more like a stout cocktail). Similarly, brewed teas like black tea or certain herbal teas (think chamomile, which has a slight bitterness) can be used as an ingredient. You can even find non-alcoholic aperitif products – for example, there are alcohol-free Italian bitter aperitivos and vermouth alternatives on the market (like a *Negroni* without the gin: use a NA gin plus a NA Italian bitter and a NA sweet vermouth). These bring the bittersweet botanical profile that usually only alcohol-based drinks had. Tonic water is another fantastic source of bitterness – its quinine bitterness can balance sweet fruit juices; try topping a mango or orange-based mocktail with tonic instead of plain soda and taste how much more complex it becomes.

- **Spice & Heat:** This is the other component that makes a drink "interesting" and slow to sip. Spice doesn't necessarily mean burning hot; it can be gentle warmth. A touch of spice gives a sensory signal similar to alcohol's burn. Ingredients like ginger, chili pepper, or warm baking spices can add that kick. Ginger can be added via ginger beer or ginger syrup (which gives a zippy spice and sweetness together). Fresh ginger muddled into a drink adds a crisp, hot note. Chili or pepper can be used very sparingly – for example, muddling a slice of jalapeño in a tropical mocktail or adding a few drops of a tincture made from chili can create a subtle heat in the throat, mimicking the warmth of a spirit. You can also use spices like cinnamon, nutmeg, clove, cardamom to add warmth (these don't burn the tongue, but they give a "warming" aromatic spice). A pinch of cayenne in a mocktail with chocolate or citrus can be exciting. Even something like black peppercorns infused in a syrup or cracked on top of a drink can contribute an unexpected spicy note. Don't be afraid to experiment here – the goal is not to make the drink painfully spicy, but just to introduce a tingle or warmth that makes the sipping experience more dynamic.

When you combine these elements – a bit of sweet, a bit of sour, a hint of bitter, and a touch of spice – you end up with a beautifully balanced mocktail that engages the full palate. For example, imagine a zero-proof version of a classic old-fashioned cocktail: you might use a non-alcoholic bourbon substitute (bringing oak and smoke flavors), a spoon of simple syrup (sweet), a couple dashes of bitters (bitter and spice), and perhaps flame an orange peel over it for aromatic citrus oils. The result is a drink that isn't "just juice" – it has depth and a slow-sipping quality very close to the original cocktail experience. Or consider a refreshing sour-style mocktail: shake up fresh lemon juice (sour) with a thyme-infused honey syrup (sweet and herbal), add a dash of grapefruit bitters (bitter and aromatic), and top with a splash of sparkling water for a bit of carbonated bite. You'll have a lovely, sophisticated drink that makes your taste buds sit up and take notice.

Another tip for complexity is using fermented or aged flavors. We already mentioned kombucha, which has a funky fermented taste that can stand in for the funk of alcohol in some recipes. Similarly, apple cider vinegar in tiny quantities can brighten and deepen a drink – some mixologists add just a barspoon of vinegar to a mocktail to give it bite. Smoke is another flavor associated with cocktails (think of smoky mezcal or peaty scotch). You can introduce a whiff of smoke by using a lapsang souchong tea (a smoky black tea) as an ingredient, or even by smoking the glass – though that's advanced technique! And don't forget salt – a little pinch of salt in a cocktail (yes, even a cocktail without alcohol) can enhance sweetness, reduce bitterness, and generally make flavors pop (just like in food). If you're doing, say, a grapefruit or cranberry mocktail that tastes a bit flat, a tiny pinch of salt can elevate it dramatically.

One more element to consider for a great mouthfeel is texture. Alcohol has a certain weight on the palate, so without it some mocktails can feel thin. You can fix this by adding small amounts of ingredients that give texture or viscosity. For instance, a teaspoon of coconut cream or a spoonful of fruit puree can add body to a tropical drink. Using a dash of aquafaba (the liquid from a can of chickpeas) or an egg white (if you're comfortable using raw egg white) in a mocktail like a sour will create a beautiful foamy head and a silky texture when shaken, making it feel indulgent. As one alcohol-free bar expert notes, one of the challenges in crafting great mocktails is ensuring the body isn't too watery, so consider incorporating a texture element like these to give the drink a satisfying weight on the tongue. A creamy ingredient (like coconut cream in a pina colada) or even something like a little spoon of yogurt in a breakfast mocktail can round out the mouthfeel.

To sum up, building flavor complexity is about balance and contrast. Don't let any one element (sweet, sour, bitter, spice) completely dominate; instead, let them play together. If you taste your drink and think, "Hmm, tasty but a bit one-note," consider what it might be lacking – maybe it needs a dash of bitters for depth, or a squeeze of lime to brighten, or a slice of ginger for kick. With practice, you'll start to instinctively know how to tweak a recipe to achieve that perfect equilibrium. The result: zero-proof drinks so layered and satisfying that no one will miss the alcohol.

Presentation & Garnish Glam

We've built our bar, mixed up some fabulous drinks, and balanced the flavors like a pro. Now for the fun finishing touches: presentation and garnishes. A well-crafted drink deserves to look as good as it tastes.

This is where you get to channel your inner stylist and make those zero-proof cocktails shine – literally and figuratively! Even though there's no alcohol, we want our beverages to have the same "wow" factor when we hand them to a guest. In this subsection, we'll explore how glassware, garnishes, and creative touches can elevate your drinks to gorgeous, magazine-spread levels of glam.

Glassware Matters: One of the simplest ways to make a drink feel special is to serve it in the right glass. Think about the difference between drinking sparkling cider out of a plastic cup versus a chilled champagne flute – the latter instantly feels like a celebration. So, consider investing in some nice glassware for your zero-proof bar. You don't need every kind of bar glass under the sun, but a selection of the basics helps: tall highball glasses for fizzy and iced drinks, short rocks/Old Fashioned glasses for more spirit-forward sips or drinks on the (large) rocks, martini or coupe glasses for elegant "up" mocktails (the ones without ice, served straight up), and perhaps some champagne flutes for bubbly non-alcoholic spritzes or celebratory toasts. Also, mugs or heat-safe glass cups are great for hot mocktails like virgin toddies or alcohol-free mulled wine. There's something psychological about holding a well-weighted glass in your hand – it tells your brain "this is a crafted cocktail, savor it." So don't hesitate to break out the fancy stemware or the tiki mugs or whatever suits the theme of your gathering. For a holiday party, you might use those cut-crystal vintage glasses you inherited; for a summer mocktail, a mason jar or a colorful glass might add whimsy. The main idea is: match the vibe of the drink with a glass that makes it feel complete.

Gorgeous Garnishes: Now onto garnishes – the jewelry of the drink. A good garnish can add aroma, flavor, and visual appeal all at once. And there are so many creative options to explore. For a start, use the fresh herbs and fruits you hopefully have stocked: a bright green mint sprig slapped between your hands to release aroma is perfect on a mojito or any citrusy cooler. A twist of lemon or orange peel adds a spiral of color perched on the rim and releases beautiful citrus oils (pro tip: twist it over the drink to spritz those oils onto the surface for extra aroma). Sugared rims or salted rims are always a hit and super easy: run a cut citrus wedge around the rim of your glass and dip it in sugar or salt (or even a spiced sugar mix like cinnamon-sugar for a holiday vibe). Suddenly your drink glass has a glistening, flavor-packed edge that looks as good as it tastes – imagine a cranberry mocktail with a rosemary-sugar rim, or a virgin margarita with the classic salt rim and a lime wheel. For holiday-themed touches, the sky's the limit: drop a couple of fresh cranberries or pomegranate seeds into a festive punch or skewer them on a cocktail pick for a pretty garnish. Use a small candy cane as a stir stick in a peppermint mocha mocktail, or toss in a cinnamon stick to a hot spiced apple drink for both flavor and decoration. In summer, edible flowers like pansies or hibiscus can float on top of a drink, or you can freeze small flowers or berries into ice cubes for a gorgeous effect. Citrus slices and wheels are always classic – a wheel of orange, a slice of starfruit, a few floating cucumber slices for a spa-like refreshment. And don't forget the power of a well-chosen straw or pick: fun paper straws in stripes or dots can add festivity (and they're eco-friendly these days), and a bamboo skewer or cocktail pick with a chunk of fruit (like a pineapple wedge and cherry for a tropical theme, or an olive for a classic vibe) tells a little story on the glass.

Fancy Ice & Eye-Catching Details: A detail that often surprises people is how much ice can affect a drink's presentation. In craft cocktail bars, you'll see beautiful crystal-clear ice cubes, oversized spheres, or even novelty shapes. Why? Because not only do they look cool (pun intended), but large ice melts more slowly, keeping drinks colder longer without diluting them quickly. As a zero-proof host, you can absolutely use this trick. Consider investing in a few large ice cube molds or sphere molds – they're inexpensive and make a big impression. Drop one big crystal-clear cube in a rocks glass for your non-alcoholic old-fashioned, and it immediately feels upscale. An expert tip from the pros: fancy ice and thoughtful garnishes "take any drink to the next level". One mixology expert specifically encourages fun ice molds not just for looks, but to *avoid watering down* your carefully crafted mocktail. You can even get creative by freezing things into your ice – imagine ice cubes with a cranberry or a mint leaf trapped inside, slowly releasing flavor as it melts, or ice made from juice or tea instead of water to add flavor as it dilutes. These little touches make your drinks not only taste great but become real conversation pieces.

Speaking of eye-catching details, have you heard of edible glitter? There are food-grade shimmer powders and glitters (often used in cake decorating) that you can add to drinks to give them a magical sparkle. A tiny pinch of edible pearl dust can make a whole punch bowl swirl with glittery clouds, delighting guests as they ladle out a cup. It's an optional flourish, but for a particularly celebratory occasion (New Year's Eve, perhaps), it can be so much fun. Similarly, you can garnish with things like gold sugar or edible gold leaf flakes to add a luxurious touch – picture a dark crimson mocktail with a gold-flecked rim for a truly show-stopping holiday drink. Smoked garnishes are another advanced trick: like torching a sprig of rosemary until it smolders, then sticking it in the drink for a rustic campfire aroma (great for a fall gathering). Or zesting fresh nutmeg on top of a frothy mocktail for a fragrant spice note right under the nose of the drinker.

The main principle of presentation is to engage the senses even before anyone takes a sip. When you hand someone a well-garnished, pretty drink, they see the colors and garnishes (sight), maybe catch a whiff of citrus or herbs (smell), feel the cold glass in hand (touch), and hear the clink of ice or a sprig as they move it (sound) – all this sets up their brain to enjoy the taste even more. You're creating a little multi-sensory experience. It shows you've put care into the drink, which makes your guest feel special. And honestly, it's just fun! There's a lot of joy to be found in picking out a perfect garnish and seeing the whole drink come together like a mini work of art.

Before we wrap up, let's not forget practicality amidst the glam. If you're hosting a larger group, you might not have time to do intricate garnishes for every single glass on the spot. In that case, consider setting up a garnish station where guests can pick their own finishing touch. You could lay out a platter with citrus twists, herb sprigs, berries, and let people customize their drinks – it becomes an interactive element of the party. Also, prep whatever you can in advance: cut your citrus wedges or twists before the party; make a batch of large ice the night before; pre-skewer some fruit garnishes on picks for easy plopping into glasses. This way you can still achieve stunning presentation without feeling overwhelmed when guests are waiting for their beverages.

In conclusion, presentation and garnish are the cherry on top (sometimes literally) of your zero-proof mixology. You've put love into the ingredients and balance of the drink, so show it off! As one alcohol-free cocktail entrepreneur enthuses, *"I love adding fun and festive garnishes, a sugar or salted rim, some fancy ice, or gorgeous glassware. It takes any drink to the next level."* Indeed, those special touches can make a simple drink feel celebratory and unique. So go ahead – rim that glass with colored sugar, float that mint leaf, clink that beautiful clear ice, and watch your guests' eyes light up. You'll know you've succeeded when people are not only saying "Cheers!" to your zero-proof creations, but also pulling out their phones to take a picture before they even take a sip. Now your zero-proof bar is fully stocked, your tools are at the ready, and your drinks look sensational. It's time to enjoy those festive alcohol-free concoctions and bask in the good vibes of inclusive, delicious celebration. Cheers to *you*, the master of the zero-proof bar!

Chapter 3

Grateful Sips – Hosting a Thanksgiving Feast, Alcohol-Free

Harvest Flavors in the Glass

A spiced autumn mocktail captures the essence of fall with cinnamon, star anise, and a sugar-crusted rim.

When crafting alcohol-free drinks for Thanksgiving, celebrate the bounty of the season by infusing each glass with autumn's signature flavors. Think spiced apple cider, velvety pumpkin purée, golden pear nectar, and tangy cranberry. These cozy, seasonal ingredients are the building blocks of delicious holiday mocktails, and they naturally echo the foods on your Thanksgiving table. Beverage experts note that many popular booze-free holiday cocktails lean on exactly these flavors – from classic apple cider and cranberries to warming spices like cinnamon and nutmeg. By using real fruit juices and purees from the fall harvest, you'll create drinks that taste like *fall in a glass* and perfectly complement your feast.

To deepen those autumnal flavors, don't shy away from warming spices and aromatic herbs. A pinch of cinnamon or nutmeg, a dash of ginger, or a drizzle of maple syrup can instantly give a drink that cozy holiday character. For example, drop a cinnamon stick into a simmering pot of apple cider or shake some pumpkin pie spice into a mocktail mix – you'll get the same comforting aroma and taste that you love in pumpkin pie or spiced lattes. Herbs from the kitchen are equally at home in your drinks: a sprig of rosemary or sage as a garnish doesn't just look festive, it also evokes the savory herbs in Thanksgiving stuffing. Incorporating these herbs and spices helps tie your beverages to the meal itself, creating a harmonious flavor experience. In fact, herb-infused sips (imagine a rosemary-spiked cider or a sage and ginger brew) can subtly mirror the earthy, savory notes of dishes like green bean casserole or roasted turkey. The result is a drink menu that feels thoughtfully tied into the season – every sip offers a little reminder of fall harvest, warmth, and gratitude.

Crucially, these zero-proof drinks deliver depth and complexity without any alcohol. Using full-bodied ingredients like cider, purees, and coconut cream (for richness) ensures your mocktails have a satisfying texture and weight on the palate, never coming off as just "juice". A splash of tart cranberry or a squeeze of citrus keeps them bright and balanced, while touches of sweetness (honey, maple, or simple syrup) round out the flavors. The goal is to craft beverages that are just as special as cocktails, minus the booze. By layering fruit, spice, and herb elements, you'll achieve that complexity. For example, an apple cider base can be enhanced with ginger and cloves for a "mulled" effect, or a pear nectar can be uplifted with sparkling water and a twist of orange to add zing. Get creative with autumn's pantry: use pumpkin butter or purée for a creamy punch, steep chai tea or mulling spices for depth, even experiment with unconventional fall produce like pomegranate or fig in your syrups. Embrace the mindset that fall flavors are your mixology toolkit. With each mocktail you mix, you're essentially bottling the cozy comfort of Thanksgiving – and your guests will taste that love in every sip.

Signature Thanksgiving Mocktails

A festive Cranberry-Orange Sparkler garnished with fresh cranberries and orange slices is perfect for toasting.

Now that we've explored the flavor palette, it's time to serve up some creative drinks! Below is a lineup of Thanksgiving mocktails that will delight your guests – each one inspired by the holiday's themes of comfort, warmth, and togetherness. From a creamy pumpkin punch to a sparkling cranberry toast, these alcohol-free recipes prove you don't need wine or whiskey to have a "spirited" celebration. Let's dive into the recipes, complete with ingredients and instructions, so you can easily recreate these festive sips at home.

Pumpkin Spice Punch

This velvety punch is a booze-free twist on classic eggnog – brimming with pumpkin pie flavor and enriched with coconut cream for a luscious finish. It's like drinking a slice of pumpkin pie with a dollop of whipped cream! Serve this in a big bowl or pitcher so guests can ladle out some creamy, spiced goodness to start the celebration. The combination of pumpkin, warm spices, and rich coconut will wrap everyone in a cozy feeling from the first sip.

Ingredients: *(Makes about 8 servings)*

- 1 cup pumpkin purée (canned or homemade)

- 1 cup full-fat coconut cream (the thick part of canned coconut milk)

- 2 cups milk or unsweetened almond milk (for a lighter punch, use dairy-free milk)

- 1/3 cup maple syrup or honey (adjust to taste for sweetness)

- 1 teaspoon pure vanilla extract

- 1 teaspoon pumpkin pie spice (blend of cinnamon, nutmeg, ginger, cloves)

- 1/4 teaspoon ground cinnamon (extra, for depth)

- Pinch of ground nutmeg (for garnish)

- Whipped cream, for topping (optional)

- Cinnamon sticks or star anise, for garnish (optional)

Instructions:

1. **Blend the base:** In a large mixing bowl or pitcher, whisk together the pumpkin purée, coconut cream, milk, maple syrup, vanilla extract, and pumpkin pie spice. Whisk vigorously until the pumpkin and coconut cream are fully incorporated and the mixture is smooth. *(Tip: You can also blend these ingredients in a blender for an ultra-smooth texture.)*

2. **Adjust flavor:** Taste the mixture and add extra sweetener if desired. The punch should taste like a creamy, liquid pumpkin pie – sweet but with a good hit of spice. If you love cinnamon, stir in the extra 1/4 teaspoon of ground cinnamon for an even warmer flavor.

3. **Chill (or warm) as preferred:** Cover the pitcher or bowl and refrigerate the punch for at least an hour before serving to let the flavors meld and to serve it chilled. *Alternatively, for a cozy twist, you can gently heat the mixture on the stovetop until warm (do not boil) and serve it as a warm punch.*

4. **Serve:** Pour or ladle the Pumpkin Spice Punch into glasses or mugs. If desired, top each serving with a dollop of whipped cream. Dust a pinch of ground nutmeg or pumpkin spice on the whipped cream. Garnish with a cinnamon stick or a star anise pod for a beautiful presentation.

5. **Enjoy:** Serve this punch as a welcome drink – its creamy texture and nostalgic pumpkin spice notes will immediately put everyone

in a festive, relaxed mood. Any leftovers can be kept covered in the fridge for up to 2 days (stir before serving again).

Cranberry-Orange Sparkler

Light, fizzy, and bursting with holiday cheer, this Cranberry-Orange Sparkler is ideal for toasting at the dinner table. It combines the tartness of cranberries with bright fresh orange, creating a drink that's refreshingly crisp. The rosy red color looks gorgeous in a champagne flute, especially with a few cranberries floating and an orange twist for garnish. With each sip balancing sweet and tart, this mocktail will have everyone saying "cheers" to a grateful gathering.

Ingredients: *(Per glass; scale up as needed)*

- 2 ounces 100% cranberry juice (unsweetened)

- 2 ounces fresh orange juice (about half an orange)

- 1 ounce simple syrup or honey (adjust to taste; you can reduce if using sweetened cranberry juice)

- 1/2 ounce fresh lime juice (for extra zing, optional)

- 3–4 ounces club soda or sparkling water (chilled) – OR use a dry ginger ale or sparkling apple cider for a sweeter, fruitier twist

- Ice cubes, for serving

- Garnish: 3-4 fresh cranberries, a half-orange slice or twist, and a sprig of rosemary or mint

Instructions:

1. **Prep the glass:** If you want a festive touch, rim the serving glass with sugar: rub a cut orange wedge around the rim and dip it in sugar mixed with a bit of orange zest. Then add a few ice cubes to the glass (a flute or wine glass works well).

2. **Mix juices and syrup:** In a cocktail shaker or mason jar, combine the cranberry juice, orange juice, simple syrup, and lime juice (if using). Add a couple of ice cubes. Shake well for about 10 seconds, until the mix is chilled. *(If you don't have a shaker, you can simply stir these ingredients in a glass with ice to chill them.)*

3. **Pour and top:** Strain or pour the cold cranberry-orange mixture into your prepared glass, filling it about halfway or a bit more. Top off the drink with 3–4 ounces of club soda or sparkling water, pouring slowly. The fizz will create a beautiful light foam and blend with the juices. Give a gentle stir to combine.

4. **Garnish and serve:** Drop a few fresh cranberries into the drink and add an orange slice on the rim (or a twist of orange peel) for visual appeal. For a lovely aroma, you can tuck a sprig of rosemary or fresh mint beside the ice – each sip will carry a hint of herbaceous fragrance.

5. **Toast away:** This sparkler is best served immediately while it's effervescent. It's a fantastic choice for the Thanksgiving toast, as the bubbly nature feels celebratory. The crisp cranberry notes also pair wonderfully with appetizers and the main meal, cutting through rich flavors (more on pairings later!). Enjoy the clink of

glasses and the knowledge that everyone can partake in the toast, young or old.

Mulled Apple Cider (Alcohol-Free)

Nothing says autumn like mulled apple cider. This warm mocktail takes the classic spiced cider and elevates it with a dash of zero-proof "bourbon" – a non-alcoholic whiskey alternative that adds smoky, oaky notes without any alcohol. You'll simmer fresh apple cider with fragrant spices until your kitchen smells like a fall wonderland. Serve it in mugs by the fireplace, and you've got a cozy drink perfect for sipping as Thanksgiving dinner winds down or while everyone relaxes. It's comfort in a cup, with a little extra complexity thanks to the bourbon alternative.

Ingredients: *(Makes about 8 servings)*

- 1 gallon fresh apple cider (unfiltered apple juice works too)
- 1 orange, sliced into rounds (plus extra orange zest for garnish, optional)
- 3 cinnamon sticks
- 6 whole cloves
- 2 star anise pods (optional, for a mild licorice note)
- 1-inch piece of fresh ginger, sliced (optional, adds a gentle zing)
- 2–4 tablespoons brown sugar or maple syrup (optional, to taste – cider is usually sweet already)

- Addition for adults: 1 cup zero-proof bourbon or whiskey substitute (non-alcoholic spirit) – optional but recommended for depth of flavor

- Garnish: Cinnamon sticks, apple slices, or orange wheels

Instructions:

1. **Combine and simmer:** In a large pot or Dutch oven, pour in the apple cider. Add the orange slices, cinnamon sticks, cloves, star anise, and ginger. Place the pot over medium heat and bring the cider just to the brink of a simmer, then reduce heat to low. Let the cider mull (warm slowly with the spices) for at least 20– 30 minutes, up to 1 hour. Do not boil the cider, as boiling can make it cloudy and boil off the delicate flavors – low and slow is key. As it simmers, the spices will infuse the cider with their aroma. (Your home will start to smell amazing – the scent of cinnamon, citrus, and apple will greet your guests at the door!)

2. **Sweeten if needed:** After about 20 minutes, taste the cider carefully (it will be hot). If you'd like it a bit sweeter or richer, stir in brown sugar or maple syrup until dissolved. The sweetness level is up to you; depending on the cider's natural sugar, you may not need any extra sweetener.

3. **Add zero-proof spirit:** In the last 5 minutes of mulling, stir in the non-alcoholic bourbon (if using). This gives the cider a subtle whiskey-like warmth and complexity, with notes of oak and vanilla, but *zero* alcohol. Important: If using an NA spirit, do not

let the cider boil after adding it – just keep it warm. (If you skip the NA spirit, your cider is completely family-friendly and delicious on its own.)

4. **Serve warm:** Ladle the mulled cider into heatproof mugs. Make sure each serving gets a bit of the orange slice or a star anise from the pot for visual appeal. Garnish each mug with a fresh cinnamon stick (guests can use it as a stirrer) or float an apple slice on top. You can also add a curl of orange zest for a burst of citrus fragrance.

5. **Sip and savor:** Serve the cider to guests gathered in the living room or around a crackling fire. This drink invites people to slow down and savor the moment. It's wonderful for those chilly November evenings – each sip is like a warm hug, with spice and apple notes enveloping your taste buds. And by using a zero-proof bourbon, everyone gets to enjoy that toasty, spiced "nightcap" feeling together, without any alcohol involved.

Pear and Thyme "Bellini"

Welcome your guests in style with this elegant yet easy Pear and Thyme Bellini. A traditional Bellini is a sparkling cocktail of prosecco and peach purée – our alcohol-free version uses autumn pears and herbal thyme to give it a Thanksgiving twist. It's light, fragrant, and bubbly, making it an excellent apéritif (pre-dinner drink) to whet the appetite. The delicate sweetness of pear paired with the aromatic oils of fresh thyme creates a beautiful balance. Served in a champagne flute, these

Bellinis feel celebratory and will make your guests feel pampered from the moment they arrive.

Ingredients: *(Per glass)*

- 2 ounces pear nectar or pear juice (if you can't find pure pear nectar, you can purée a very ripe pear and strain it)

- 1/2 ounce fresh lemon juice (about 1 tablespoon, to brighten the pear's sweetness)

- 1 teaspoon honey or simple syrup (pear is mild, so a touch of sweetness helps, adjust to taste)

- 3–4 ounces sparkling apple cider **or** club soda (well-chilled)

- 1 sprig of fresh thyme

- Garnish: Additional thyme sprig and a thin slice of fresh pear

Instructions:

1. **Infuse the thyme:** In a small cup or the base of your flute, gently muddle the sprig of fresh thyme with the honey (or simple syrup) and lemon juice. Press just enough to bruise the thyme leaves – this releases their oils and flavor. You don't need to pulverize it; a gentle press and twist a few times will do. This creates a quick thyme-infused syrup in the glass.

2. **Add pear nectar:** Pour the pear nectar into the glass and give it a light stir to mix with the thyme, lemon, and honey. At this point, you have a fragrant pear-thyme base. If you prepared this in a

separate cup (for easier muddling), transfer the mixture to a champagne flute now.

3. **Top with bubbles:** Slowly top up the glass with sparkling apple cider or club soda. Pouring against the side of the glass can help retain more bubbles. Aim for about 3 to 4 ounces, or until the glass is almost full. The drink will turn a delicate golden color.

4. **Garnish:** Thread a thin slice of pear onto the stem of the thyme sprig (this makes a lovely combined garnish) and place it into the glass. The thyme sprig will also continue to infuse the drink as you sip. Alternatively, you can simply float a small pear slice on top of the drink and add a fresh thyme sprig for looks.

5. **Serve immediately:** The Pear and Thyme Bellini is best enjoyed while the carbonation is lively. Hand these to your guests right as they arrive. It's a sophisticated alternative to champagne – all of the sparkle, none of the alcohol. The gentle sweetness and herbaceous note help set a relaxed, cheerful tone. As your friends take their first sips, they'll notice how the garden-fresh hint of thyme plays against the sweet pear – a signal that this evening will be full of thoughtful touches and delicious surprises.

Each of these signature mocktails ties into Thanksgiving themes of comfort and warmth. The Pumpkin Spice Punch wraps you in creamy spiced nostalgia; the Cranberry-Orange Sparkler adds a bright, toast-worthy clink to the gathering; the Mulled Cider brings literal warmth and spice; and the Pear Bellini offers a light, elegant welcome. By offering a variety – some bubbly, some creamy, some hot, some chilled – you ensure that every guest, from grandparents to kids, finds something to enjoy. And the best part? All these drinks are alcohol-free, so everyone can savor them freely. These recipes show that a festive holiday cocktail experience doesn't require any gin, wine, or whiskey – you can mix up plenty of holiday spirit using just the flavors of the season.

Feast-Friendly Pairings

Crafting delicious mocktails is only half the story – the other half is serving them in harmony with your Thanksgiving feast. Just like wine pairings, well-chosen alcohol-free drinks can elevate the dining experience by complementing each dish. Here are some feast-friendly pairing tips to make your menu sing, course by course:

- **Pre-Dinner Welcome Mocktail:** Start the celebration the moment guests walk in. Have a signature pre-dinner drink ready to break the ice and tantalize taste buds. For example, greet everyone with the Pear and Thyme Bellini or a small glass of the Pumpkin Spice Punch. The light, bubbly pear mocktail awakens the palate without filling people up, while the creamy pumpkin punch offers cozy nostalgia in sippable form. Serving a special alcohol-free aperitif like this sets an inclusive tone from the get-go – everyone has something festive in hand as you all mingle. To make it easy on yourself, you can prepare a big batch in advance: fill a dispenser or punch bowl with a make-ahead mixed mocktail (perhaps a double batch of that Pumpkin Spice Punch or a sparkling cider-based concoction) so guests can serve themselves as they arrive. This self-serve drink station not only encourages people to mix and mingle, but it also frees you, the host, to attend to last-minute kitchen needs or join the conversation.

- **During the Feast – Pairing with Savory Dishes:** As you sit down to the turkey and all the trimmings, pair your dishes with drinks that enhance those rich, savory flavors. Tart, cranberry-based mocktails are a natural fit with roast turkey – the tangy fruit notes act like a palate cleanser, cutting through the richness of gravy and buttered sides. For instance, the Cranberry-Orange Sparkler we described not only provides a refreshing contrast to succulent turkey and creamy mashed potatoes, but its hint of citrus also echoes the cranberry sauce on the table, tying flavors together. Meanwhile, a spicy ginger-pear tonic can be a surprising star alongside herb-heavy dishes like stuffing or roasted vegetables. The ginger's heat and pear's sweetness complement savory herbs (think sage, thyme, rosemary in your stuffing) in a delightful way – it's a balance of sweet, spice, and herb that brings out the best in those dishes. You can create such a tonic by mixing pear nectar with ginger beer and a squeeze of lemon, garnished with a sprig of thyme to match the seasoning of the food. Also consider serving a light, fizzy drink during the meal – something with citrus or effervescence – as a continuous palate refresher. Even a simple blend of sparkling water with a splash of orange and a few pomegranate seeds can do wonders between bites of creamy casseroles and cheesy gratins, keeping everyone's taste buds awake. The key is to provide options: set pitchers of water infused with lemon and mint, maybe a jug of chilled apple cider, and your selected mocktails on the table. Guests can then choose sips that complement each course. By thoughtfully matching flavors (cranberry with turkey, ginger with herbs, citrus with heavy gravies), you turn the drink menu into another set of "side dishes" that elevate the whole feast.

- **Sweet Finale – Dessert & Drinks:** Don't let the pairing fun stop at dessert! Thanksgiving desserts, especially spiced classics like pumpkin or pecan pie, pair wonderfully with drinks that mirror their flavors. A warm mug of mulled apple cider (from our recipe or simply kept simmering on the stove) is an excellent choice to serve with dessert – the cinnamon, clove, and orange notes in the cider bring out the pumpkin pie's spice and the apple in apple pie, creating a harmonious sweet ending. Alternatively, you can offer hot chai tea lattes or cinnamon-dusted hot cocoa for a cozy, caffeine-free companion to pies and cakes. For an inventive twist, consider a dessert mocktail like a Pumpkin Pie Frappé. This blended treat is essentially pumpkin pie in a glass: imagine cold pumpkin-spice latte meets milkshake. *Here's a quick recipe:* blend 1/2 cup pumpkin purée, 1 cup vanilla ice cream (or frozen coconut dessert for dairy-free), 1 cup milk or almond milk, a tablespoon of maple syrup, and a pinch of cinnamon and nutmeg. Puree until smooth and frothy. Serve in small mason jars or glasses with straws, topped with whipped cream and a sprinkle of graham cracker crumbs to mimic pie crust. The pumpkin pie frappé is indulgent, so small portions are best – but it will make eyes light up, especially for kids or anyone who saved room for "drinkable dessert." The goal for your finale drink is to echo the dessert flavors: if it's pumpkin pie, go for pumpkin or spice in the drink; if it's apple crisp, perhaps a cold sparkling apple cider with a scoop of sorbet; for chocolate desserts, a peppermint hot chocolate might hit the spot. By matching sweet with sweet, you reinforce those beloved flavors and end the meal on a perfectly coordinated note.

- **Hosting Tip – The Self-Serve Punch Bowl:** To make your life easier during the party (and to encourage guests to feel at home), set up a self-serve drink station. For example, you can prepare a large Thanksgiving punch in a beautiful bowl or drink dispenser and let everyone refill as needed. One idea is a Cranberry Harvest Punch: combine cranberry juice, apple cider, a sliced orange, and a handful of cranberries in a big pitcher with lots of ice; top it with club soda or ginger ale for fizz. This kind of big-batch mocktail means you're not playing bartender all night. Place the station in an accessible spot, with pretty glasses and a bucket of ice, plus a ladle if using a punch bowl. You might also leave out little tags or a menu card describing the drink and suggesting food pairings ("Great with turkey and ham!") for a fun touch. Not only does this free you up to enjoy your own party, it also creates an interactive element as guests gather around mixing drinks and chatting. Everyone can try their hand at topping up a glass, and it often becomes a conversational centerpiece. A self-serve station underscores that *mi casa es su casa* vibe – guests will feel welcome to help themselves, and you get to circulate and actually participate in the festivity.

By thoughtfully pairing each stage of your Thanksgiving feast with an appropriate alcohol-free drink, you ensure that the flavors of food and beverage complement each other like a well-choreographed dance. Tart drinks brighten up rich bites, spicy sips play up savory herbs, and sweet finishes enhance dessert spices. The payoff? A meal where every element, from the toast to the dessert, works in harmony – and no one misses the alcohol one bit.

Cozy Atmosphere & Traditions

A memorable Thanksgiving is about more than food and drink – it's about the atmosphere and the traditions that bring people closer. Hosting alcohol-free naturally steers the gathering toward wholesome, cozy activities and ensures everyone, young and old, feels included. Here's how to create that warm, inviting vibe for your zero-proof Thanksgiving celebration:

Start with a gratitude ritual: Since Thanksgiving is all about thankfulness, consider beginning your feast (or before dinner) with a gratitude toast. Invite everyone to raise their alcohol-free drink – be it a sparkler or a simple soda – and share one thing they're especially thankful for this year. *"This Thanksgiving, raise a glass and toast to what you're grateful for, booze-free,"* as one lifestyle publication aptly puts it. This moment can be heartwarming and set a positive, reflective tone for the evening. You'll find that clinking glasses of cider or mocktail in thanks feels just as festive as champagne, if not more so, because everyone can fully participate in the sentiment. Some families even make this a yearly tradition, with each person speaking in turn. There might be laughter, maybe a few happy tears, but the feeling of solidarity and gratitude is palpable. By doing this with zero-proof sips, you ensure the kids at the table or those who don't drink alcohol are equally part of the tradition – no one is having to toast with an inferior option like plain water. It's a beautiful way to kick off the gathering and remind everyone of the true spirit of the holiday.

Cozy touches for the senses: Create an environment that wraps your guests in comfort. Little details can make a big difference in how the evening feels. For instance, keep a simmering pot of spiced cider or mulling spices on the stove throughout the event. Not only can guests ladle themselves a warm drink from it, but it also fills your home with an inviting aroma of apples, cinnamon, and cloves that instantly says "holiday" when people walk in. Soft lighting is another element of coziness – think candles on the mantel or warm-hued string lights around the dining area (flameless candles are a safe alternative if kids are around). In the background, have a gentle soundtrack playing: perhaps soft jazz, acoustic folk, or classic holiday tunes at a low volume. This music sets a relaxed mood and gives a pleasant backdrop to conversations without overpowering them.

Create spaces for relaxation: After the big meal, everyone tends to drift toward the living room or a comfortable area. Arrange comfy seating with extra pillows and throw blankets, inviting guests to literally and figuratively "settle in." Encourage people to grab a cozy seat with their dessert or post-dinner drink. Maybe set up a "mocktail lounge" corner where you have a small station of after-dinner options – a carafe of decaf coffee, the pot of warm cider, maybe some peppermint tea or hot chocolate packets – so people can pick their favorite nightcap to sip. This gives the same sense of winding down as a liqueur or whiskey by the fire might, but with herbal tea or cider. Dim the overhead lights a bit and let the glow of lamps or the fireplace (if you have one) add to the ambiance. The idea is to signal that the hectic part of hosting is done; now it's time to relax and enjoy each other's company.

Plan fun, inclusive entertainment: Without a focus on drinking, you can steer the post-dinner activities toward classic, wholesome entertainment that suits all ages. Break out the board games, card decks, or a puzzle on the coffee table. A little friendly competition in Charades or a round of Pictionary can get everyone laughing and interacting. If games aren't your family's thing, queue up a beloved holiday movie that everyone can watch together – something light that can play in the background while conversations continue, or a nostalgic film that draws people in. The goal is to replace "booze-fueled antics" with bonding moments. Often, in alcohol-heavy parties, folks might splinter off or some might overindulge leading to drama or tiredness. Here, with everyone sober, the focus naturally shifts to activities that create memories. You'll notice people stay engaged longer into the evening, since no one is zoning out or getting sleepy from alcohol. Maybe set up a gratitude jar or a Polaroid selfie station for fun, or go outside for a brisk starlight walk if weather permits – anything that brings joy and connection.

Embrace the drama-free spirit: One of the huge benefits of hosting an alcohol-free Thanksgiving is the peace of mind that comes with it. As the night goes on, you can relax knowing that nobody will have one drink too many. There's less chance of misunderstandings or heated arguments that sometimes occur when wine flows freely. Instead, you get to see the best of everyone – fully present, happy, and comfortable in their own skin. Guests often comment on how refreshed they feel when leaving an event like this. In the absence of alcohol, people tend to stay more *in the moment*: conversations are lively and genuine, the kids can play without the adults turning rowdy, and every guest will remember the night clearly the next day. You, as a host, have essentially guaranteed a safe space for all. By the end of the celebration, as you're maybe enjoying one last cup of tea or a final bite of pie, you'll notice the uniquely cheerful, calm energy in the room. Laughter comes easily, smiles are sincere, and there's a collective contentment that is truly priceless. When it's time to say goodbye, you can be confident that everyone will drive home safely or head to bed without any spins – and that the holiday memories made will remain crystal clear for everyone. In the days that follow, those memories – of heartfelt toasts, delicious drinks, shared games, and warm hugs – will shine bright, unclouded by anything but happiness.

In closing, an alcohol-free Thanksgiving feast is all about inclusion, flavor, and genuine connection. By serving delightful zero-proof drinks and setting a cozy scene, you allow all your guests to fully participate in every toast, every laugh, every tradition. The focus shifts to what truly matters: the gratitude we share and the good times we create together. And as the host, you get the joy of knowing you provided an experience where everyone felt welcome and left uplifted. These "grateful sips" and the atmosphere around them ensure that your Thanksgiving is not only feast-filled and festive, but also safe, supportive, and memorable for all the right reasons. Cheers to a holiday celebration that's high in spirit, minus the spirits!

The ideas and tips in this chapter were informed by experts and enthusiasts who celebrate the possibilities of zero-proof mixology. Holiday mixologists emphasize using seasonal fruits, spices, and even products like pumpkin butter to craft festive alcohol-free drinks. It's well documented that popular non-alcoholic holiday cocktails lean on classic flavors like eggnog, apple cider, cranberry, and warm spices. Food writers encourage offering a variety of nonalcoholic drinks at big gatherings so everyone has something special to sip – not just soda or water. Pairing suggestions draw from mindful drinking guides, which note that herbal or tart mocktails can beautifully complement Thanksgiving dishes (a cranberry-sage spritz with turkey, or a rosemary-infused lemonade with savory sides, for example). Hosting guides also recommend setting up non-alcoholic drink stations with juices, garnishes, and custom options to engage guests in the process. As Southern Living puts it, *"raise a glass and toast to what you're grateful for, booze-free"* – a sentiment that captures the inclusive spirit of a zero-proof celebration. Finally, health and wellness sources remind us that without alcohol, we stay more present to savor every shared memory, which means your Thanksgiving will likely end on a high note of clear-headed happiness. All these insights underscore one message: a holiday without alcohol can be every bit as festive, flavorful, and full of camaraderie – perhaps even more so, when the focus is on gratitude and connection. Enjoy your Zero-Proof Thanksgiving to the fullest!

Chapter 4

Merry & Bright (Without the Buzz) – Alcohol-Free Christmas Celebrations

The Christmas season sparkles with traditions – twinkling lights, familiar carols, and the comforting aroma of cinnamon and pine. Holiday celebrations often center around warming drinks and festive toasts, but enjoying a merry & bright Christmas doesn't require a drop of alcohol. In fact, more and more people are embracing alcohol-free celebrations, and hosts are finding creative ways to keep the holiday spirit high without the buzz. With a bit of imagination, you can offer all the classic flavors of Christmas in zero-proof form, ensuring everyone – from kids to grandparents – can join the cheer.

Reimagining Classic Christmas Drinks

There's a special nostalgia in the drinks we savor each December, from creamy eggnog by the fire to spicy mulled wine at Christmas markets. Reimagining these classic Christmas beverages in non-alcoholic versions is easier than you might think. The key is to capture the flavors and coziness of the originals, using clever substitutes for spirits. For example, you can whip up a velvety eggnog that's every bit as rich and satisfying as the traditional version – minus the rum. A base of milk (dairy or almond) simmered with vanilla, nutmeg, and cinnamon yields that same creamy holiday treat, especially with a dollop of whipped cream on top and a sprinkle of nutmeg for aroma. Likewise, a mug of mulled "wine" can be made using fruity juices like pomegranate or dark grape warmed gently with mulling spices (think cloves, cinnamon sticks, star anise, and orange peel). The result is a ruby-red, spiced punch that's just as warming as the real deal, filling your home with the scent of Christmas.

Classic cocktails also have their place in holiday lore, and these too can be transformed. Love the snap of peppermint schnapps in a cocktail? Try a Peppermint Mocha Mocktini – a playful alcohol-free twist that blends peppermint and chocolate flavors for a minty-sweet delight, without any liqueur. It delivers the same candy-cane coolness and mocha richness in a sophisticated glass. Cravings for a hot toddy on a frosty night can be satisfied with an herbal tea toddy: brew strong spiced herbal tea (like ginger or cinnamon tea), add a squeeze of lemon and a drizzle of honey, and you have a throat-warming, spiced drink that feels just as soothing as its whiskey-laced cousin. Holiday mocktails often echo Christmas classics – from creamy eggnogs and hot toddies to spiced ciders and peppermint sippers – simply without the alcohol. With a few clever ingredient swaps (a splash of rum extract here, a spice infusion there), nobody has to miss out on the taste of Christmas. Each sip carries the nostalgic flavors of the season – creamy sweetness, warm spices like nutmeg and cinnamon, and refreshing peppermint – all with the bonus of a clear head and an inclusive atmosphere.

Festive Holiday Mocktail Recipes

To bring these ideas to life, here are a few star mocktail recipes tailored for the Christmas season. These drinks are as festive to look at as they are delicious to drink, proving that holiday beverages can feel special without any alcohol involved. Each recipe includes a description of its flavor profile and serving style, inspiring you to get creative with presentation and garnishes. Feel free to dress up your drink station with elegant punch bowls, sparkling glassware, and plenty of holiday flair – half the fun of a good mocktail is how you serve it!

Candy Cane Cooler: A creamy, minty delight that tastes just like a candy cane in a glass. The Candy Cane Cooler combines refreshing peppermint with luscious white chocolate and a hint of vanilla. It's a sweet, indulgent drink that evokes the fun of Christmas candy, perfect for dessert or as a party welcome drink. Serve it chilled in a glass rimmed with crushed candy canes for extra flair, and watch it shimmer like fresh snow.

Ingredients:

- 1 cup milk (peppermint-flavored milk, or regular milk heated with crushed candy canes until dissolved, then chilled)

- 1/2 cup white chocolate chips or white chocolate syrup

- 1/2 cup heavy cream (or coconut milk for a dairy-free option)

- 1 teaspoon vanilla extract

- Crushed ice

- Whipped cream and additional crushed candy cane for garnish

Instructions:

1. In a saucepan over low heat, combine the milk and white chocolate chips, stirring until the chocolate melts and infuses the milk with creamy sweetness. Let this mixture cool.

2. Stir in the heavy cream and vanilla extract. (For a stronger peppermint flavor, you can add a drop or two of peppermint extract or some of the melted candy cane syrup.)

3. Fill a cocktail shaker or large jar with crushed ice. Pour in the cooled mixture and shake well until frothy and chilled.

4. Strain into chilled glasses. Serving tip: Before pouring, rim each glass with crushed candy cane (use a bit of syrup or honey on the rim to make the candy cane pieces stick). Top each glass with a swirl of whipped cream and a pinch of crushed candy cane for a festive, snowy look.

A bright Cranberry Ginger Fizz mocktail with a frosty rosemary sprig and sugared cranberries, capturing the look of a miniature Christmas wreath.

Cranberry Ginger Fizz: This sparkling crimson mocktail is tangy, spicy, and utterly Christmas-y. A blend of tart cranberry and zingy ginger gives the Cranberry Ginger Fizz its refreshing bite, while a splash of bubbly soda adds effervescence. The flavor profile balances sweet-tart cranberry with a warm ginger kick – imagine a cross between ginger ale and a cranberry spritz, dressed up for the holidays. It's typically served in a highball or rocks glass over ice, garnished generously to resemble a little Christmas tree in each glass.

Ingredients:

- 1/2 cup 100% cranberry juice (unsweetened for a tarter drink, or cranberry cocktail for a sweeter one)

- 1/2 cup ginger ale or ginger beer (ensure it's non-alcoholic; ginger beer will be spicier)

- 1/4 cup fresh orange juice (for a citrusy note that rounds out the flavor)

- 1 teaspoon honey or simple syrup (optional, to adjust sweetness)

- Ice cubes

- Garnish: Fresh rosemary sprigs, fresh cranberries, and orange slices

Instructions:

1. Fill a glass with ice cubes. Pour in the cranberry juice and fresh orange juice. Give it a gentle stir to combine the fruit juices.

2. Top off the glass with ginger ale or ginger beer, pouring slowly. The drink will turn a festive bright red and start to fizz. If you prefer a sweeter profile, stir in a teaspoon of honey or simple syrup until dissolved.

3. Now for the festive finish: thread a few cranberries onto the base of a rosemary sprig (the rosemary's shape and green color make it look like a tiny evergreen branch). Place the sprig in the glass so it stands up amid the ice – it will look like a miniature Christmas tree in your drink! Add an orange slice on the rim or

floating in the liquid for a pop of contrasting color and a hint of Christmas citrus.

4. Serve immediately while it's bubbly.

A creamy Non-Alcoholic Eggnog Latte topped with fluffy whipped cream, a dusting of nutmeg, and a cinnamon stick – capturing the cozy essence of Christmas.

Non-Alcoholic Eggnog Latte: All the decadent flavor of classic eggnog, transformed into a warm latte-style drink with zero alcohol. This latte is rich and velvety, spiced with nutmeg and cinnamon, and has a lovely froth that makes it feel like a treat from a coffee shop – except there's no espresso unless you choose to add it. The flavor profile is traditional eggnog: think creamy vanilla custard notes (without actual eggs in this version), plenty of holiday spices, and a sweetness that's warming but not overwhelming. By using almond milk and coconut milk, this recipe is friendly to those who avoid dairy, yet it still satisfies eggnog cravings. Serve it in mugs with a cinnamon stick stirrer and a cloud of whipped cream, and you have a drink that invites everyone to slow down and savor the moment.

Ingredients:

- 2 cups almond milk (or dairy milk, if preferred)

- 1 cup canned coconut milk (for richness; or use half-and-half or oat creamer for a dairy version)

- 3 tablespoons sugar (or maple syrup, to taste)

- 1 teaspoon pure vanilla extract

- 1/2 teaspoon ground nutmeg (plus more for garnish)

- 1/2 teaspoon ground cinnamon

- Optional: 1/4 teaspoon rum extract (to mimic the flavor of rum without alcohol)

- **Optional coffee twist:** 1/2 cup strong brewed coffee or 2 shots decaf espresso (if you want a true "latte" with coffee flavor, but this is entirely optional)

- Whipped cream (for topping)

Instructions:

1. In a saucepan, combine the almond milk and coconut milk. Heat on medium, stirring occasionally, until the mixture is steaming (do not let it fully boil to prevent scorching).

2. Whisk in the sugar (or maple syrup), vanilla extract, ground nutmeg, and ground cinnamon. If using rum extract for that traditional nog note, add it now. Continue to heat gently for a few minutes, allowing the spices to infuse. The kitchen will start to smell like a Christmas bakery – sweet and spicy.

3. If you want to include the coffee element (for an *eggnog latte* in the modern sense), pour in the brewed coffee or espresso and stir. Otherwise, skip this step for a purely creamy spiced nog without the coffee.

4. Once everything is heated and well combined, use a whisk or immersion blender to froth the mixture slightly (you can also carefully transfer it to a blender, then return to the pan – or simply whisk vigorously by hand). Frothiness gives it that latte feel.

5. Pour the hot eggnog latte into mugs. Top each with a generous swirl of whipped cream. Finish with a dusting of nutmeg or cinnamon on top, and drop a cinnamon stick into each mug as a fragrant stirrer. Serve warm and enjoy slowly. Each sip is like a hug of holiday flavor – creamy, spiced, and comforting – without any alcohol to weigh you down.

Hosting the Jolly Gathering

Throwing a Christmas party with zero-proof flair is an opportunity to get extra creative and put activities and togetherness at center stage. Here are some festive theme ideas and tips for hosting a jolly gathering that everyone will remember:

- **Ugly Sweater Mocktail Party:** Embrace the goofy charm of ugly Christmas sweaters by making it the theme of your alcohol-free soirée. Encourage guests to don their tackiest holiday sweaters. Set up a mocktail bar for guests to mix creative drinks, or even have each person bring a favorite zero-proof concoction to share. Offer a prize for the ugliest sweater to get everyone laughing. Between the outrageous outfits and the inventive drinks, there's plenty of fun conversation that doesn't involve alcohol.

- **Cookie Exchange & Mocktails:** Combine two of the sweetest holiday traditions – cookies and festive drinks – into one gathering. Host a cookie exchange where each guest brings a batch of their favorite Christmas cookies to swap. Pair the treats with complementary mocktails for a truly indulgent experience. For example, serve spiced apple cider or a snickerdoodle "milk punch" (a creamy milk-based spiced mocktail) alongside cinnamon sugar cookies, or a bright Candy Cane Cooler with peppermint bark brownies. A rich non-alcoholic eggnog latte goes wonderfully with nutmeg-infused shortbread. Set out elegant punch bowls or dispensers for each drink, labeled with fun names, so guests can help themselves as they sample cookies.

- **Hot Beverage Bar for a Winter's Night:** For an evening gathering, especially on a cold winter night, create a cozy hot drinks bar. Think of it as a warming station for guests coming in from the snow. You can have large carafes or slow-cookers keeping drinks warm: one with velvety hot cocoa (with marshmallows, candy canes, and whipped cream as toppings), another with mulled cider steeped in spices, and perhaps a pot of decaf coffee or a holiday herbal tea like peppermint or spiced chai. Let guests build their own perfect hot drink – some might add a scoop of cocoa to their coffee for a mocha twist, others might mix cider and tea. Provide mix-ins like cinnamon sticks, cloves, citrus slices, and flavored syrups. This interactive setup not only caters to all ages (kids will love making their own hot chocolate creations, and adults will enjoy the gourmet coffeehouse vibe) but also fills the air with incredible aromas.

No matter what style of gathering you choose, consider the timing and structure that best fits a booze-free celebration. A holiday brunch can be delightful – you could host a Christmas brunch featuring mock mimosas (mix orange juice with sparkling white grape juice for a bubbly, morning-friendly toast) or poinsettia mocktails (cranberry juice with ginger ale or sparkling cider). Daytime events naturally carry less expectation of alcohol, making it easier for families to take part.

On the other hand, an evening soirée can be made special with a signature alcohol-free punch as the centerpiece (for example, a large bowl of shimmering cranberry-citrus punch with floating fruit and spices). In the evening, plan plenty of festive activities so the focus stays on fun: organize a round of Christmas caroling in the neighborhood, set up a station for trimming the tree or decorating ornaments together, or play lighthearted party games like Christmas movie trivia. When guests are engaged in these activities, they're not thinking about what's missing in their glass – they're simply enjoying the holiday spirit.

Finally, lean into beloved traditions to carry the gathering. Sing "Silent Night" by candlelight, have everyone share something they're grateful for this year, or do a classic White Elephant gift exchange. These moments create a sense of togetherness that becomes the highlight of the event. Without the fog of alcohol, laughter is brighter and conversations more memorable. You'll find that a party focused on connection and holiday joy naturally minimizes any focus on the absence of alcohol – there's just too much else to relish.

Spreading Cheer for All Ages

One of the greatest benefits of alcohol-free Christmas celebrations is that they can include **everyone**, from the youngest child to the oldest adult. No one feels left out, and the festive drinks and activities can be enjoyed by all ages. Here's how to make sure your festivities spread cheer across the whole crowd:

Start by offering fun, inclusive drinks that kids, teens, and non-drinking adults alike will adore. A big bowl of "Santa's Punch" can be a showstopper – imagine a bright red punch bowl filled with a mixture of cranberry, cherry, and pineapple juices, sparkling water or ginger ale for fizz, and slices of oranges and strawberries floating like jewels. Ladle it into cups for the little ones and watch their eyes light up at the name and the flavor. It's a flavorful fruit punch with a holiday twist, and it ensures that children have something special to toast with while adults enjoy it too. Set up a sparkling cider bar with flutes of chilled apple or grape cider garnished with fresh fruit, so even the kids and teens can raise a festive toast. When it's time for everyone to clink glasses, they can all join in – no Champagne needed – and the moment feels magical for all.

To make younger guests feel grown-up and appreciated, pay attention to presentation. Kids notice when their drink is just as pretty as the cocktails the adults might have had. So serve Shirley Temples or other mocktails in nice glassware (maybe skip the most fragile crystal for the littlest hands, but there are plastic stemmed glasses that look the part). Add garnishes that are fun and safe – a candy cane hooked over the edge of a cocoa mug, a rim of green and red sugar on a punch glass, or a tiny snowman-shaped stirrer in a cup of milk punch. Teenagers often enjoy the chance to try more "adult" flavors too, so you could include options like a virgin mojito (mint, lime, and soda) or the peppermint mocha mocktini mentioned earlier, and serve it in a chic martini glass for sophistication. When everyone, regardless of age, has a festive drink in hand, it creates a sense of shared experience and belonging.

What about guests who might *expect* the usual beer, wine, or cocktails? The good news is that with a well-planned alcohol-free menu, most people find they don't even miss the booze. Be upfront (in a friendly way) when inviting people that you'll be serving amazing holiday mocktails – set a positive tone by saying you're excited for them to try your "holiday creations" or "secret recipe punch." When guests arrive, greet them with a particularly delightful alcohol-free welcome drink (like a steaming cup of spiced pomegranate mulled punch or a frothy eggnog latte) so they immediately have something tasty in hand. Often, the ambiance and flavors will speak for themselves. If someone casually asks for a beer or wine out of habit, simply smile and mention you have something even better. Offer them a top-up of the flavorful punch or a fresh glass of whichever mocktail they were enjoying. Most will be pleasantly surprised at how complex and satisfying a well-made mocktail can be. After a couple of cheers and rounds of rich conversation, the absence of alcohol truly becomes a non-issue.

The overarching message of *Zero-Proof Celebrations* is this: removing alcohol doesn't remove the magic of the holidays. In fact, it can often heighten it – without anyone overindulging, everyone stays bright-eyed and fully present (and awake to open presents in the morning!). The focus shifts from the drinks per se to the *people* and the moments shared. And those moments, in the end, are what make the season truly bright. When your gathering wraps up, guests will leave remembering the laughter, the creativity of the drinks and games, and the warmth of being together. They'll realize – as you will – that the true spirit of Christmas thrives on connection and joy, no spirits required. Cheers to celebrations that everyone can cherish!

Chapter 5

Countdown to Midnight – A Hangover-Free New Year's Eve

N ew Year's Eve is the grand finale of the holiday season – a night of glittering parties, countdowns, and joyous toasts. Traditionally, those midnight celebrations have been drenched in champagne and cocktails, but an exciting shift is happening. More party hosts are discovering that you can ring in the New Year with all the sparkle and fun, minus the alcohol (and minus the next-day headaches). In fact, sales of non-alcoholic beverages have surged in recent years, reflecting a growing movement toward festive zero-proof celebrations. This chapter shows you how to throw a dazzling New Year's Eve bash where every clink of the glass comes with good taste and zero regret. Let's countdown to midnight with style, flavor, and everyone included – and wake up on New Year's Day feeling fantastic.

Bubbly Without Booze

Nothing says "New Year's Eve" like popping a bottle of bubbly at midnight. The good news is, you don't need alcohol to keep that tradition alive. There's now a world of alcohol-free sparkling wines, ciders, and bubbly tonics that deliver all the effervescence and celebratory feel of champagne. For years, non-drinkers made do with overly sweet sparkling grape juice or cider – the kind kids sip at parties. Those can work in a pinch, but today's zero-proof "champagnes" are on another level, often so crisp and authentic that guests hardly miss the booze. Many premium alcohol-free sparkling wines are crafted from real wine grapes, brewed and then gently de-alcoholized, so they retain the complex flavors of the vineyard without the punch of alcohol. The result? You can pour something golden and fizzy into everyone's flute, and every toast feels just as special.

Recommended Sparkling Alternatives: An array of excellent alcohol-free bubbly brands await your New Year's toast. One top pick is *Noughty Alcohol-Free Sparkling Chardonnay*, praised for its dry, velvety flavor with notes of apple and peach – impressively close to the real thing. If you prefer a Spanish flair, try *Rondel Zero* (a de-alcoholized cava); it comes in a cork-topped bottle with gold foil and offers a balanced, crisp finish that rivals traditional cava. For a classy German option, *Leitz Eins Zwei Zero Sparkling Riesling* delivers lively citrus notes and a hint of Riesling's signature aroma, all with 0.0% alcohol. And of course, there's nothing wrong with popping open a bottle of sparkling cider. A high-quality cider – think crisp sparkling apple or pear juice – brings familiar sweetness and fizz that families have loved for generations.

In recent years, innovative botanical tonics have also joined the party. For example, *TÖST*, a sparkling white tea infused with white cranberry and ginger, is marketed as a "lovely champagne alternative to toast the New Year," offering a lightly sweet taste with a dry finish so it feels adult and refined. With choices like these, every guest – from the wine lover to the teetotaler – can have something bubbly in hand when the clock strikes twelve.

Serving in Style: Part of what makes champagne special is the ritual: the *pop* of the cork, the elegant flute glasses, the bubbles rising as everyone gathers to toast. Your alcohol-free bubbly can deliver all of that. Many non-alcoholic sparkling wines come in full-size champagne bottles that open with a festive *pop!* (be ready with a towel, as some are as fizzy as the real deal). Pour your chosen drink into chilled champagne flutes or vintage coupes to elevate the experience – presentation is key. You might garnish each glass with a twist of lemon or a few fresh pomegranate arils (which float like ruby-red jewels in the bubbles) for a fancy touch. When midnight approaches, gather everyone, pour the "champagne" or cider, and let the countdown begin. As glasses clink together, no one will be feeling left out or "less than" – the effervescence and the moment are what matter. You're proving that a toast without alcohol can still feel utterly sparkling and celebratory.

Zero-Proof French 75: One fabulous New Year's mocktail to try is a booze-free spin on the classic French 75 champagne cocktail. The traditional French 75 mixes gin, lemon, sugar, and champagne – we'll keep the flavor but skip the liquor. Start with a quality alcohol-free gin (many distilleries now make gin alternatives packed with botanical flavor). Shake the gin substitute with a squeeze of fresh lemon juice and a dash of simple syrup, then strain it into a champagne flute. Instead of champagne, top it off with chilled sparkling lemonade or a dry non-alcoholic sparkling wine. The result is a *Zero-Proof French 75* that's bright, bubbly, and elegant. Garnish with a curl of lemon peel spiraling inside the flute. This drink looks just like the real deal and tastes citrusy and refreshing – perfect for a midnight toast with a twist.

Sparkling Pomegranate "Champagne" Cocktail: For a festive option that literally *sparkles*, try a pomegranate-based mocktail that mimics a celebratory champagne cocktail. In a shaker or pitcher, combine pomegranate juice with a splash of orange or cranberry juice and a squeeze of lime. Add a few drops of orange blossom water or a sprig of rosemary to infuse a subtle aroma (this adds complexity, so the drink feels grown-up). When ready to serve, pour this bright crimson blend into champagne flutes and top each with a generous pour of alcohol-free sparkling cider or wine. The star of the show: drop a few pomegranate arils into each glass. They'll dance in the bubbles and catch the light, giving a jewel-like, glittering effect in the glass. For extra flair, you can even sprinkle a pinch of edible gold glitter on top. This *Sparkling Pomegranate "Champagne"* cocktail tastes tart-sweet and looks incredibly celebratory. Hand these out and watch everyone's eyes light up – it turns the simple act of raising a toast into a moment of New Year magic.

Glamorous Zero-Proof Cocktails

New Year's Eve is the perfect occasion to go all-out with glitz and glamour – and that applies to the drinks, too. Just because a cocktail has no alcohol doesn't mean it can't be a showstopper. In fact, zero-proof mixology is all about creativity and presentation. For the year's biggest party night, consider crafting an array of glamorous mocktails that look as impressive as their boozy counterparts (if not more so). Think of it as giving your guests all the luxe, festive vibes of a swanky cocktail party – without any alcohol in the mix.

For instance, wow your crowd with a Golden Glow Martini, a concoction as bright as New Year's fireworks. This drink gets its radiant gold color and subtle spice from ginger and turmeric – ingredients that also add a warm, earthy flavor. You might mix a ginger-turmeric syrup or shrub (easily made by simmering fresh ginger, a pinch of turmeric, sugar, and water) with a squeeze of lemon and top it with ginger ale or club soda. Serve it in a classic martini glass. The result is a vivid golden mocktail that practically glows; a thin slice of candied ginger or a twist of orange makes the perfect garnish on the rim. Not only does the Golden Glow Martini taste zingy and invigorating, it also looks ultra-glam – a drink fit for ringing in the new year with style.

Another stunner is the Blackberry No-jito Royale, a fancy twist on the classic mojito that swaps rum for extra fun. Start by muddling ripe blackberries, fresh mint leaves, and a bit of sugar or honey in a shaker – this releases the berries' deep purple juice and the mint's refreshing oils. Add freshly squeezed lime juice and ice, then shake (omitting any alcohol, of course). Pour this sweet-tart, minty base into a tall glass or even a champagne flute. Now make it a "Royale" by topping off the drink with something sparkling: a splash of club soda or, to amp up the elegance, some alcohol-free sparkling wine. The fizz brings it all to life. Drop in a few extra whole blackberries and a sprig of mint for a gorgeous garnish. The Blackberry No-jito Royale is bursting with color and flavor – it feels festive and upscale, yet it's completely alcohol-free.

Adding Theatrical Flair

What makes a cocktail truly glamorous often comes down to the theatrical touches. Don't hold back on garnishes and presentation; New Year's is the night to be a little "extra." Edible glitter and gold? Yes, please. You can rim the glasses of your mocktails with edible glitter or colored sugar to give them a dazzling sparkle when they catch the light. Consider adding whimsical surprises to the drinks: for example, freeze berries or edible flowers into ice cubes so that as they melt, lovely floral and fruity notes are released while looking beautiful. And for the ultimate touch of luxury, float a tiny piece of 24-karat edible gold leaf on top of a cocktail – it's an extravagant detail that will make your guests feel like royalty. One expert in zero-proof entertaining notes that fun garnishes, special ice, and gorgeous glassware can truly "take any drink to the next level", and New Year's Eve is the perfect stage for that kind of showmanship.

Lighting and presentation can also add drama. If you have them, pull out your most eye-catching glassware: cut-crystal coupes, tall flutes, or martini glasses with unique stems. You might garnish drinks with flamboyant elements like a curled citrus peel, a skewered slice of starfruit, or a sprinkle of edible star-shaped confetti on the surface. Little details like drink tags or glamorous picks can further dress up the beverages. Set up a well-lit "mocktail bar" area at your party where these jewel-toned creations can be displayed – people will gather around just to admire (and Instagram) the drinks. The goal is to create an atmosphere where the lack of liquor is never noticed; what guests see are vibrant, glittering cocktails that promise celebration in every sip.

Batching Upscale Mocktails

Of course, on New Year's Eve the host should be having fun too – not stuck shaking drinks all night. The key is batching your cocktails in advance so you can relax and enjoy the festivities. Many mocktails can be made in large batches; you can prepare pitchers or dispensers of your base mixes ahead of time. Here are some tips for batching your zero-proof cocktails without sacrificing quality or sparkle:

- **Pre-chill everything:** Chill your ingredients (juices, sodas, mixers) well in advance, and keep your prepared mocktail mixes refrigerated. This way, your big batch of drinks starts out cold and requires less ice (which means less dilution).

- **Add bubbles last:** If your recipe calls for a carbonated component like club soda, ginger beer, or alcohol-free sparkling wine, don't mix that in until you're ready to serve. Pour the base of the mocktail into glasses first, then top each with the fizzy element. This ensures every drink is bubbly and fresh.

- **Garnish in advance:** Prep garnishes ahead of time to make assembly easy. Thread berries or citrus twists onto cocktail picks, have mint sprigs washed and ready, and rim glasses with sugar or glitter just before the party. When it's go-time, you can simply pour and garnish without fuss.

- **Self-serve setup:** Consider setting out a self-serve mocktail station. Place a filled pitcher of your signature mocktail (or two different ones for variety) on a table with an ice bucket, glasses, and a tray of garnishes. Guests can help themselves to refills. This not only frees you up, but it also lets people mingle and play bartender in a fun way.

By batching drinks, you maintain that upscale feel – cocktails ready in beautiful pitchers or punch bowls can even add to your décor – and you won't miss a beat of your party. Instead of juggling shakers at 11:55 p.m., you'll be on the dance floor or counting down along with everyone else, glass in hand.

The Inclusive Midnight Toast

When the final seconds of the year tick down, it's time for the big toast – and everyone should be able to participate in that magical moment. One wonderful aspect of hosting a zero-proof New Year's Eve is how inclusive it can make the midnight toast. No one is left empty-handed or feeling excluded because they "aren't drinking." Some of your guests might be sober by choice, others could be expecting moms, designated drivers, or even kids allowed to stay up late – and *every* one of them can raise a beautiful glass of something sparkly and delicious. As one alcohol-free celebration expert reminds us, the tradition of holiday toasts "shouldn't just be reserved for those drinking alcohol" – the clinking of glasses and sharing of hopes for the New Year is a ritual everyone deserves to enjoy.

To make this happen, plan ahead to ensure you have enough festive non-alcoholic drinks for all ages. You might stock up on bottles of sparkling grape juice or cider specifically for the children or anyone who loves a sweeter option. At 11:55 p.m., start pouring out those drinks into champagne flutes (plastic ones are fine for little hands) so that when the countdown begins, you can distribute them quickly. It can help to announce a few minutes before midnight: "Grab your glass, we're getting ready to toast!" – that way nobody misses out. The image of a crowd where grandparents, teenagers, and toddlers alike are all holding shimmering drinks, eyes bright with excitement as the countdown reaches "3...2...1!", is truly heartwarming.

Inclusive Toasting in Action: Consider the example of the Nguyen family, who turned their New Year's toast into a multigenerational tradition. They host a gathering every year with relatives spanning four generations, and when it's time for the toast, they hand out sparkling juice in flutes to everyone – from Great-Grandpa down to the youngest cousins.

One year, as the clock struck midnight, the family all cheered and clinked glasses. Grandma and her seven-year-old grandson gently tapped their flutes together and shouted "Cheers!" The boy beamed, thrilled to be part of the grown-up ritual, and Grandma later remarked that it was the most meaningful toast of her life because *everyone* was included. This anecdote shows how the simple act of offering non-alcoholic champagne or cider to *all* guests can make the symbolism of the New Year's toast even more powerful. The moment becomes less about alcohol and more about togetherness – exactly as it should be.

Remember, a toast is about togetherness and hope for the future – ultimately, the contents of the glass are secondary. By ensuring every guest has something special to sip, you're honoring the spirit of the toast itself. You might even encourage guests to share a thought or a single word for the New Year as you toast (making sure everyone has a drink to raise). These inclusive midnight toasts often turn out to be the highlight of the party, full of laughter, maybe a few happy tears, and definitely memories that will be treasured long after the night.

New Year, Fresh Start – Next-Day Perks

Ending the night without alcohol doesn't just feel good in the moment – it feels fantastic the next morning. One of the best rewards of a hangover-free New Year's Eve is waking up on January 1st clear-headed, refreshed, and ready to seize the day. Traditionally, many New Year's Day mornings are lost to people sleeping in late, nursing headaches, or groaning "Never again" as they regret those last few cocktails. In fact, statistics show that New Year's Day is often the most hungover day of the entire year. But that *doesn't* have to be you or your guests. By choosing zero-proof drinks, you're sidestepping the classic New Year's hangover and giving yourself a head start on the year ahead.

Imagine this: instead of a fuzzy morning and a queasy stomach, you awaken on New Year's Day full of energy. You might get up early to watch the first sunrise of the year with a cup of hot coffee, or rally a few friends for a brisk New Year's Day hike in the crisp winter air. Perhaps you'll throw on some music and cook a big, hearty brunch – actually *enjoying* the first meal of the year rather than just using it as hangover fuel.

You'll find that the memories of your New Year's Eve are crystal clear, too. You'll laugh about the jokes shared at 11 p.m., scroll through photos on your phone that are all in focus, and relish the fact that you rang in the year fully present in each special moment.

This ties right into the "new year, new you" mindset. Starting the year without a hangover is a gift to yourself. It's so much easier to launch into those New Year's resolutions – whether it's hitting the gym, beginning a new project, or simply embracing a more mindful lifestyle – when you're feeling well-rested and positive on Day One. Many people even choose to do "Dry January" as a wellness challenge, and by celebrating New Year's Eve alcohol-free, you've already got a jump-start on that goal. As one survey noted, 79% of people who rang in the New Year sober were happy to wake up without a hangover on January 1st– no surprise there! You get to skip the pain and start the year with a smile.

Ultimately, a hangover-free New Year's Eve sets a tone of wellness and intention for the months ahead. You prove to yourself that you don't need alcohol to mark a milestone or have a fantastic time. Your January 1st is spent not in recovery, but in enjoyment – perhaps going for that early jog, tidying up while humming "Auld Lang Syne," or writing down some goals for the year while the memories of the joyful night are still fresh. And the best part? You're not losing any of the fun. The party you hosted was brimming with laughter, music, delicious drinks, and cheer – everything a great New Year's Eve should have – plus the bonus that nobody has to suffer for it the next day.

As you step into the New Year, take pride in having celebrated in a mindful, inclusive, and healthy way. You've welcomed the next chapter of life with clarity and optimism. After all, there's no better way to begin a fresh year than by feeling your best. With that zero-proof midnight toast, you've started your year off on the right foot – bright-eyed, hangover-free, and ready to embrace all the opportunities that the coming year will bring. Cheers to that, and Happy New Year!

Chapter 6

Mix and Mingle – Party Planning Tips for Any Celebration

Welcome to the world beyond the winter holidays! In this chapter, we'll explore how to take your zero-proof entertaining skills year-round. From seasonal recipe swaps to creative party themes and stress-free serving hacks, you'll learn to host festive alcohol-free gatherings for any occasion. The goal: make every guest feel included and ensure everyone leaves remembering the fun and camaraderie – not what was (or wasn't) in their glass.

Adaptable Recipes Year-Round

A festive Cranberry Thyme Spritzer garnished with fresh thyme springs – all the sparkle and flavor of a holiday cocktail, without the alcohol.

One of the joys of zero-proof mixology is how adaptable it is. The delicious drinks you mastered for the holidays can be *tweaked* for beachy summer cookouts, spring baby showers, autumn tailgates – you name it. The principle is simple: swap in seasonal ingredients and keep the tasty core of the recipe. For example, that cranberry-thyme spritzer your guests loved at Christmas can turn into a strawberry-basil spritzer on July 4th with just a few ingredient changes. Tart cranberry juice and woody thyme suited winter; ripe strawberries and fragrant basil scream summer. The result is the same refreshing sparkle, but with flavors that fit the season.

Seasonal Swap Ideas: Once you get the hang of it, you can remix recipes endlessly. Here are a few ideas to spark your creativity:

- **Winter to Summer:** A spiced cranberry punch from December can become a Berry Basil Fizz in July. Swap cranberries for muddled raspberries or strawberries, and rosemary or thyme for fresh basil. You'll still get a gorgeous ruby-red drink, but with a sunny berry sweetness instead of winter spice. *Hint:* The cranberry-thyme spritzer pictured above has all the festive bubbly, red "cocktail" vibes – a Whole30-friendly treat. For summer, puree strawberries with a squeeze of lime, add sparkling water, and garnish with basil for a totally new twist that's just as crowd-pleasing.

- **Fall to Spring:** Love your autumn apple cider mocktail with cinnamon? Turn it into a light spring brunch punch by mixing in iced green tea, a splash of elderflower syrup, and swapping cinnamon sticks for sprigs of mint. Suddenly that cozy fall drink is a refreshing Apple-Mint Iced Tea Spritzer fit for a sunny day. Or take a pumpkin-spice flavored drink from Halloween and serve it over ice with vanilla and cold brew for a *pumpkin spice "iced latte" mocktail* at a springtime coffee-themed gathering.

- **Holiday to Everyday:** Your Christmas pomegranate-thyme "mimosa" (pomegranate juice + ginger ale + thyme) can transform into a Sunday brunch special by using orange or pineapple juice, club soda, and a pinch of fresh mint. The idea is the same – fizzy fruit goodness – but now it's a tropical morning treat. In our kitchen, mulled cranberry cider (with cloves and cinnamon) became a chilled Cranberry Citrus Cooler in summer just by serving it over ice with lemon slices.

Don't be afraid to mix-and-match elements once you've mastered a few base recipes. Zero-proof mixology is wonderfully forgiving. Try a new herb here, a different fruit juice there. One creative home bartender shared that after she concocted a simple cranberry-thyme spritzer to lift her Christmas spirits, she immediately started dreaming up new combos: *"Rosemary-grapefruit? Cilantro-lime with a pinch of salt? Oh, the possibilities!"*. That's the beauty of it – once you have the basics down, every season and occasion is an opportunity to invent a new favorite drink.

The Year-Round Spritzer

Here's a quick recipe adaptation:

Recipe: Holiday Cranberry Thyme Spritzer (makes 1 serving) *Ingredients:* 2–3 sprigs fresh thyme, 2 oz pure cranberry juice, 6 oz club soda, crushed ice, sweetener to taste (optional). *Instructions:* In a glass, muddle one thyme sprig to release its flavor. Fill the glass with crushed ice. Add cranberry juice, then top with club soda. Stir gently. Garnish with another thyme sprig. Sip and feel the holiday cheer!

Summer Twist: To make a Strawberry Basil Spritzer, swap out the thyme and cranberry. Muddle 2 fresh basil leaves and 2 sliced strawberries in the glass instead of thyme. Use 2 oz strawberry puree or juice in place of cranberry juice (add a squeeze of lime for zing), then top with club soda and ice. Garnish with a basil leaf and a juicy strawberry slice. Now you have a *red-and-green* mocktail that's ironically perfect for Christmas and a hot July afternoon! Different vibe, same mix-and-mingle appeal.

- *Seasonal tip:* Use what's fresh. In summer, that might be watermelon, cucumber, berries, melon, or stone fruits. In fall, think apple, pear, cinnamon, ginger. Spring loves herbs like mint, basil, lavender, and floral touches. By tuning into the seasons, you'll naturally come up with swaps: e.g. a cranberry mule with ginger beer (great for winter) can become a peach ginger cooler in summer by using peach nectar and iced ginger tea.

- *Color and Garnish:* Adaptable recipes aren't just about taste – consider color and presentation. A rosemary sprig garnish that looked like a Christmas tree in December can be replaced by a sprig of mint or an edible flower in spring. Red and green cranberries and thyme gave a holiday look; for a Halloween party you might use blackberries and a twist of orange peel for an orange-and-black "spooky" spritzer. Little changes in garnish instantly customize the drink's theme.

The big message: zero-proof entertaining isn't just for the winter holidays. You now have the skills to whip up festive drinks in every season and for any reason. Birthday parties, baby showers, backyard BBQs, Sunday brunches, even a random Tuesday night can all be celebrations with the right alcohol-free drink in hand. Once you start experimenting, you'll find you can tailor any recipe to any occasion. Your creativity is the only limit. Cheers to a year full of flavorful, alcohol-free toasts!

Creative Themes & Décor

A huge part of party atmosphere is the theme and decor. When you're hosting alcohol-free, a fun theme and inviting decor go a long way to set the mood (guests won't even think about the missing booze when they're dazzled by the ambiance). Let's talk about dreaming up themes, activities, and decorations that pair perfectly with zero-proof hosting.

Embrace Fun Themes: Think beyond the standard holiday decor – *any* gathering can have a playful theme that ties the night together. How about hosting a "Mocktail Mix-Off" competition? This can work for a variety of occasions – a spring fling, a girls' night in, even a bridal shower. Invite each friend to invent an alcohol-free drink on the spot (provide a table of juices, syrups, herbs, and garnishes as the "palette"). Everyone gets to be a mixologist for the night. I once attended a friend's birthday party where they did exactly this: each guest created a custom mocktail inspired by the birthday girl's personality! There were hilarious presentations, from a bubbly cotton-candy garnished drink representing her whimsical side, to a bold spicy ginger mocktail symbolizing her fiery humor. We laughed, we sipped all the crazy concoctions, and the act of inventing drinks became the game of the night. In the end, the birthday girl crowned a winner (and we all begged for the recipe of "Jenny's Cardamom Rose Mocktail" – a gorgeous orange-pink creation with a rosewater and strawberry base). A Mocktail Mix-Off theme turns the absence of alcohol into a *highlight* – the creativity and friendly competition steal the show.

Another idea: throw a tropical mocktail luau in summer. Transport your guests to a beach paradise with alcohol-free tiki drinks. Serve virgin piña coladas or mango-coconut "sunset" smoothies in coconut cups. Mix up a big bowl of Luau Punch – a classic Hawaiian-inspired fruit punch with pineapple, orange, and lemon-lime fizz. (One family shared that this slushy pineapple-orange "luau punch" is their go-to for summer gatherings and birthdays.) Dress up your space with faux palm leaves, tiki torches or string lights, and hand out leis at the door. Play some Hawaiian or beach tunes. The tropical flavors and upbeat decor will make everyone feel like they're on vacation – no rum needed. For an extra touch, freeze pineapple rings and maraschino cherries into an ice ring and float it in the punch bowl to keep it cold and pretty. If a few guests *do* want a boozy option, you can set a bottle of rum to the side for self-service – but truthfully, when we did our last luau party, hardly anyone touched it because the mocktails were so satisfying.

Adaptable Décor: You don't need a closet full of party decorations for every holiday. Instead, **repurpose versatile decor pieces** to fit your theme. A few examples:

- **String Lights:** Twinkling string lights are your best friend. They instantly add warmth and magic to any space. Drape fairy lights around your living room for a cozy winter gathering, hang them under your patio umbrella for a summer evening party, or wrap them around a banister or trees for ambiance. White or warm-yellow lights work year-round – you can then add accent colors via other decor. (Some hosts even fill clear lanterns or jars with a tangle of string lights for a makeshift "glowing centerpiece".) The great thing is these lights create a magical ambiance for any occasion – from an intimate bridal shower to a backyard birthday. They provide that soft, welcoming glow *without* relying on a booze-fueled haze.

- **Candles & Lanterns**: Likewise, candles add atmosphere in all seasons. Use unscented votives or LED candles on tables for a gentle glow (scented ones can clash with drink aromas). You can easily change the look by placing them in seasonally-themed holders: try red and green votive holders for Christmas, pastel glass for spring, or rustic wood candle holders for a fall harvest vibe. One thrifty tip: repurpose mason jars as candle holders, maybe with a ribbon or a few themed trinkets tied around the rim (orange and black ribbon for Halloween, burlap for a farmhouse theme, etc.). Lanterns (metal or paper) are also fantastic – fill a lantern with string lights or a pillar candle and some faux leaves/pinecones in autumn, or ornaments in December, then swap in seashells or flowers come summer. This way, the same set of lanterns or jars can be reinvented each party.

- **Floral Arrangements:** Flowers aren't just for spring. You can adapt floral decor to any celebration. For example, a simple arrangement of white daisies or baby's breath looks lovely for a baby shower or spring brunch. Add small flag picks or red, white, and blue ribbons, and that bouquet becomes a July 4th centerpiece. In fall, you might fill a vase with sunflowers and wheat stalks for Thanksgiving, or insert a few mini pumpkins around a floral foam ring. In winter, evergreen sprigs with red berries (or cranberries) in water make a beautiful, seasonally-scented arrangement. The key is to use what's in season or matches your party's palette. Don't hesitate to borrow from nature – colorful autumn leaves, blooming branches in spring, etc., can be used in centerpieces at no cost.

Color Schemes: A super adaptable decor strategy is to change up accent colors while keeping basic items neutral. For instance, invest in some plain white or metallic-gold tablecloths, plates, and string lights. Then tailor the color accents: red and green napkins, balloons, or flowers for Christmas; orange and black for Halloween (with maybe some fake cobwebs on those string lights!); pastels for Easter or a baby shower; gold and silver for New Year's glam. Even something as simple as swapping throw pillow covers or adding a themed banner can signal a holiday. Guests walk in and immediately know "Oh, it's a fall party!" because you have pumpkins, orange fairy lights, and brown burlap runners on the table. For a New Year's party, you might use the same string lights and candles as Christmas, but add silver confetti, glittery "Happy New Year" signs, and swap red poinsettias for metallic tinsel garlands. These little decor tweaks are inexpensive but totally set the scene.

Activity Stations & Ambiance: When alcohol isn't the focal point, put something else fun at the center of your party. We love DIY stations – they get people moving around and mingling. Besides the mocktail bar (more on that below), consider a DIY photo booth corner. It's easier than it sounds: hang a festive sheet or shimmering curtain as a backdrop, put a basket of goofy props (hats, costumes, signs) nearby, and let guests snap photos with their phones. You can even set up a tablet or camera on a tripod with a remote if you want to be fancy. This gives guests an activity that loosens everyone up *without any liquor*. I've seen fully sober wedding receptions turn into absolute blast *simply because* they had a silly photo booth and everyone was trying on wigs and oversized sunglasses! It's proof that laughter and playfulness – not liquor – create the best memories.

Music is another huge ambiance setter. Craft a themed playlist to match your party. If it's a tropical luau, throw in plenty of reggae, Hawaiian, or beachy tunes. For a 1920s-themed party, go for jazz and swing. A holiday party? Some classic carols and upbeat winter hits (just watch the tempo if you want dancing vs. chatting). One dry wedding planner noted that music becomes even more essential without the "social lubricant" of cocktails – it brings people together and keeps energy flowing. So put thought into your soundtrack; a great playlist gets guests tapping their feet, singing along, maybe even dancing, *totally forgetting that they don't have a drink in hand.* And if they *do* have a drink in hand, it'll just make them want to toast with their tasty mocktail and dance more!

Lastly, encourage interactive elements. An interactive mocktail bar (discussed next section) can be the theme *and* decor centerpiece – think a gorgeous display of colorful juices, fruit, and herbs that doubles as edible decor. Other interactive ideas that pair well with zero-proof hosting: a *garnish-your-own cupcake* station at a birthday (who needs a champagne toast when you have a cupcake decorating contest?), a *cocoa bar* at a winter gathering (guests customize hot chocolates with toppings), or a *"barista" station* with fancy coffees and teas for an alcohol-free brunch. These engage guests and create an atmosphere of abundance and activity, so nobody is left twiddling their thumbs or wondering "where's the bar?". The bar is there – it's just serving delicious zero-proof creations and inviting everyone to participate.

In short, by choosing a creative theme and decorating thoughtfully, you set an ambiance where alcohol simply isn't missed. Whether it's a Mocktail Mix-Off, a tropical luau, a retro soda shop vibe with root beer floats and a jukebox, or a cozy game night with fairy lights and board games, your party will have a clear identity and focus. Guests will be too busy enjoying the theme – snapping photos, grooving to music, tinkering with garnishes – to even think about asking for a drink refill of anything stronger. You're not just hosting a sober party; you're creating an immersive experience. And *that* is what they'll remember.

Serving Hacks & Drink Stations

As the host, you want to enjoy the party too – not be stuck shaking drinks all night. The key is to set up self-serve stations and clever prep hacks so that the event runs itself (almost!). Here we'll cover practical tips: DIY drink stations, big-batch mixing, keeping drinks cold and labeled, and other tricks to keep your celebration stress-free and *Instagram-worthy*.

Self-Serve Mocktail Bar: Setting up a serve-yourself drink station is a game-changer for any party. Not only does it free you from playing bartender, it also encourages guests to mingle as they mix. Here's how to do it:

- Pick a spot – a bar cart, a table, or a section of the kitchen counter – and turn it into the mocktail station. Gather everything a guest might need to fix themselves a drink. This means glasses, ice, mixers, garnishes, and tools all laid out neatly. Arrange it attractively: fruit slices in little bowls, herbs in a small vase or on a tray, colorful syrups in dispensers or bottles, stacks of pretty glasses, fun paper straws or cocktail picks in a jar, etc. The setup itself becomes part of the decor.

- Batch your recipes. Prepare one or two large pitchers or dispensers of a *signature mocktail* in advance. For example, you might fill a big drink dispenser with that strawberry-basil spritzer or a citrusy punch. Add fruit slices and herbs inside for visual appeal. If it's a carbonated drink, you can add the bubbles (club soda, ginger ale, etc.) at the last minute to keep it fizzy. Label the dispenser with the drink's name (e.g. *"Summer Berry Splash"*) and ingredients. Now guests can simply pour themselves a glass. Bonus: Have a second dispenser of plain iced water or a mild flavored water (like cucumber-mint or lemon water) for anyone who wants to alternate or dilute drinks.

- DIY recipe cards: In addition to the pre-made pitcher, it's fun to let guests create their own concoctions (especially if you're doing the Mix-Off contest!). Provide a couple of easy recipe cards or signs at the station. For instance, frame a card that reads: *"Build Your Own Mocktail: 1) Pick a juice (orange, cranberry, etc.), 2) Add a splash of syrup (grenadine, honey, etc.), 3) Top with something bubbly (soda, ginger beer), 4) Garnish!"* When people see this, it gives them permission to play. You can also list a few simple combos to inspire them: *Citrus Sparkler = OJ + lemon + club soda; Berry Fizz = muddled berries + a squeeze of lime + ginger ale*, etc. These guidelines empower guests to mix drinks to their taste, and it becomes a conversational activity ("Hey, did you try the cucumber mint spritz? What did you put in yours?").

- Essential tools at hand: Make sure to supply basic bar tools to make mixing easy. A couple of muddlers (or wooden spoons) for mashing fruit/herbs, a jigger or measuring cup for those who want exact ratios, a small shaker or two if anyone wants to shake a drink with ice, and stirrers or spoons. Have a bowl or bucket for discarding used garnishes or excess, and plenty of napkins or towels for little spills. It sounds like a lot, but you likely have these around the kitchen – and having them out means guests aren't hunting through your drawers. Everything is accessible, and clearly labeled if possible.

Here's a handy checklist to set up your drink station like a pro:

Self-Serve Drink Station Checklist:

- **Big-Batch Mocktails:** At least one large pitcher or dispenser of premixed mocktail ready to pour (e.g. a punch or signature drink).

- **Mixers & Bases:** An assortment of juices, sodas, flavored sparkling waters, kombucha, iced tea, etc., for mixing. Include sugar-free or diet options (club soda, diet ginger beer) for those watching sugar.

- **Fresh Ingredients:** Bowls of cut citrus (lemons, limes, oranges), berries, cucumber slices, mint, basil, etc. – these serve as mix-ins *and* garnishes. (Tip: Keep extra in the fridge to refill as they get low.)

- **Syrups & Sweeteners:** Set out a few fun syrups like grenadine, honey or agave, simple syrup, maybe vanilla or herbal syrups. Don't forget a natural zero-calorie sweetener (stevia drops or similar) for sugar-free folks. Label each bottle.

- **Garnish Tray:** A tray or platter with garnish picks like cocktail umbrellas, toothpicks with cherries, cocktail rims (e.g. salt, sugar, chili for spicy mocktails). Even put out a jar of edible flowers or a shaker of cinnamon – these *little extras* make the bar feel special.

- **Tools & Glassware:** Muddler, bar spoon, measuring jigger, small shaker, strainer – and a variety of glasses (tall, short, champagne flutes for "fizz" drinks, mugs if hot drinks). If you expect kids, include some plastic cups or fun sippy cups.

- **Ice Station:** A big ice bucket filled with ice (or use an insulated cooler hidden under the table). Pro-tip: use large ice cubes or an ice ring in punch bowls for slow melting, so drinks don't dilute quickly Have tongs or an ice scoop handy. Consider flavored ice

– freeze mint leaves or berries into some cubes for those who want to use them as garnish.

- **Signage:** Little chalkboard labels or cards naming each drink or ingredient. Clearly mark anything that's diet/light or caffeine-free. For example, label one pitcher *"Spiced Pear Punch (Alcohol-Free)"* and another *"Iced Hibiscus Tea – Caffeine-Free"*. This helps guests navigate choices confidently. A cute sign that says "Zero-Proof Bar – Mix and Mingle!" or "Help Yourself to a Mocktail" also sets a welcoming tone.

By checking these off, you've anticipated guests' needs. They can serve themselves with ease, and you're freed up to actually talk to your friends and enjoy the shindig.

A refreshing Strawberry Basil Spritzer bar set-up: fresh berries, herbs, and citrus allow guests to get creative with their zero-proof drinks.

Make-Ahead Hacks: Preparing things before guests arrive is a lifesaver. Aside from batching drinks, prep garnishes and mixers ahead. You can squeeze citrus juices hours before and keep in jars in the fridge. Wash and trim herbs and fruits so they're ready to go. If you plan to muddle something like mint or basil for each serving, consider making a muddled concentrate: e.g. muddle a bunch of basil with some sugar and lime juice, keep that in a small jar, and guests can spoon a bit into their glass instead of muddling per drink. For any syrup-based drink, you can mix the syrup and juice components in advance (without the soda) – that way guests just combine the premix with ice and soda.

Punch Bowls & Dispensers: Never underestimate the power of a good punch bowl. Punch is the original party drink, after all! Find a pretty bowl (or a beverage dispenser with a spout) and fill it with your feature mocktail. It becomes a visual centerpiece as well as the drink source. People gravitate toward it. You can even freeze a decorative ice ring for it: for example, in a ring mold or Bundt pan, layer some fruit (citrus slices, berries) and water or juice and freeze. Float this "ice wreath" in the punch to keep it cold and gorgeous. Because it's large ice, it will melt slowly – *hack:* a slower melt means your punch stays flavorful longer, a trick many mixologists use for cocktails too. One host at a housewarming party raved that her huge ice ring with oranges and cherries not only looked great but kept the punch chilled perfectly.

If using a dispenser, a tip: put a few slices of fruit or cucumber *inside* the dispenser with the drink for flavor and appearance, but also keep a long spoon nearby in case the spout clogs with fruit – it happens. And don't fill the dispenser to the brim; leave some air gap especially if it's carbonated, so it doesn't overflow with fizz.

"Mocktail Kits" Around the Venue: Here's a fun idea if you have a larger space or many guests: set up multiple mini drink stations or "mocktail kits" in different spots. Maybe one table has the makings for a No-jito (virgin mojito) – think a tray with a pitcher of limeade, a bowl of mint leaves, a bottle of club soda, and recipe card saying "Mix 3 parts limeade + 1 part soda, add mint, voila!" Another corner could feature a "Sparkling Bar" – a spread of flavored sparkling waters or alcohol-free bubbly, with fruit purees or juices to top them off (guests can make faux bellinis or mimosas). You could even theme them: a "Coffee Mocktail" station with cold brew, cream, vanilla, etc., to make things like cold brew "martinis" or mocha shakes – great for a brunch or late-night dessert cocktail vibe. By scattering these stations, you avoid crowding in one spot and encourage people to circulate ("Have you tried the drink over at the patio table yet? It's a DIY Italian cream soda!").

Keep It Cold: Warm, flat soda or lukewarm punch is no fun – so plan for ice and chilling. Aside from ice cubes, chill your mixers ahead of time (put sodas, juices in the fridge the night before). Use insulated pitchers or punch bowls if you have them. For an outdoor party in heat, consider placing your punch bowl inside a larger bowl of ice or nest it in a cooler of ice. Also, slow-melting ice cubes (like big cubes or spheres) can keep individual drinks cool longer without as much dilution. If you really want to get fancy, there are silicone molds for large ice cubes or spheres that fit into glasses – a talking point for sure. But an easy hack is just freezing water in a cleaned yogurt container or similar to make a big ice chunk for the punch bowl. It works!

One more trick: chill your glassware. If you expect a big rush at the start, pop some glasses in the freezer 30 minutes before the party. A frosty glass makes that mocktail feel extra "cocktail-y" when poured. Similarly, keep wine glasses or champagne flutes in the fridge for sparkling cider or bubbly grape juice toasts.

Label, Label, Label: We touched on this, but clear labeling is so important that it bears repeating. You might know which pitcher is the virgin sangria and which is the sweet tea, but guests won't unless you tell them. Use tags, tent cards or even cute hanging labels on drink dispensers. Identify what the drink is (*"Citrus Punch"*) and optionally highlight that it's non-alc (*"0% alcohol"* or a playful note like *"All flavor, no booze"*). This not only manages expectations but also reassures designated drivers or non-drinkers that *every* option on that table is safe for them. Consider also labeling key ingredients especially for those with dietary concerns: e.g. *"contains nuts (orgeat syrup)"*, *"caffeine-free"*, or *"sugar-free – sweetened with stevia"*. One mocktail catering company advises dividing the station into sections for large events and using clear signage so guests can navigate with ease. The last thing you want is someone hesitating because they're not sure what's in a drink or mistaking the spicy ginger beer for an alcoholic brew. Good labeling is part of good hospitality – it silently answers guests' questions so they feel confident and included.

By using these serving hacks, any party – whether a swanky New Year's Eve or a casual backyard cookout – will run smoothly. You'll find that guests love the freedom of a self-serve bar ("It makes it feel like a fun interactive cocktail experience," one guest told me at a dry event, marveling at all the garnish choices). Meanwhile, you get to circulate and enjoy the festivities instead of constantly refilling cups. And here's a secret: people *love* taking photos of beautifully presented drinks. Your thoughtfulness with the mocktail bar may very well end up on social media feeds, with guests proudly posting their colorful creations. Stress-free for you, and social-media-worthy for them – that's a win-win.

Welcoming Every Guest

The hallmark of a truly great host is making every single guest feel comfortable. When hosting zero-proof celebrations, inclusive hospitality is more important than ever. You'll likely have a diverse crowd – from health-conscious friends to those who usually drink at parties. The goal is to anticipate their needs and ensure nobody feels left out or disappointed. In this section, we'll cover how to offer inclusive drink options (vegan, low-sugar, caffeine-free, etc.), how to handle guests who might ask about alcohol (or want to BYO), and tips for keeping the focus on the fun rather than the alcohol. With a bit of planning and confidence, you can make your event welcoming to all.

Offer Variety for Dietary Needs: Just as you might cater the food to vegetarians or people with allergies, do the same with drinks. Think about what your guests might appreciate:

- **Vegan-Friendly Drinks:** Most of our mocktails will naturally be vegan (fruits, juices, herbs). But watch out for ingredients like honey (common in many syrup recipes) or dairy (some creamy mocktails might use milk or ice cream). Have substitutes ready: for instance, offer agave or maple syrup as alternatives to honey so vegan friends can enjoy the same drinks. If you're doing something like a "nog" or creamy punch, consider using almond milk, coconut milk, or oat creamers so that non-dairy guests are covered. A "Coconut Nog" made with coconut milk and winter spices can be just as rich as one with eggs and dairy. Label any creamy punch clearly if it contains dairy vs. plant-based milk.

- **Low-Sugar or Keto Options:** Not everyone wants a sweet drink. Some may be watching their sugar or carb intake (diabetics, keto dieters, or just the health-conscious). Include at least one low-sugar mocktail option. This could be as simple as a sparkling water with fresh lemon and mint (no added sugar), or an unsweetened iced herbal tea with berries. Kombucha is another great low-sugar, probiotic option that feels festive and tangy without loads of sugar. You can also use natural zero-calorie sweeteners in some drinks: e.g. a stevia syrup in a lemonade or using diet ginger ale for mules. One health site recommends choosing a nutritious base beverage like kombucha, seltzer, or unsweetened green juice to build mocktails that won't spike blood sugar. You might make a pitcher of "Green Garden Spritz" – a mix of cucumber, lime, and mint infused water with a splash of kombucha – which looks lovely and has almost no sugar. Or provide sodas like Diet Sprite/Cola and let guests add a dash of fruit juice so they control sweetness. Having these choices ensures those who need to limit sugar can still sip something fun.

- **Caffeine-Free Choices:** If your party is in the evening, be mindful that some guests avoid caffeine (especially older guests or those who don't want to be up all night!). Many sodas and teas have caffeine, so provide caffeine-free alternatives. Decaf iced tea or herbal tea-based punches (hibiscus, chamomile, etc.) are fantastic – for instance, an iced hibiscus-berry punch has a deep red color and tart flavor, totally caffeine-free. Sparkling water and fruit juices are obvious caffeine-free staples. If you're serving coffee or tea later (common at dessert), include decaf options. For a winter party, have decaf coffee and perhaps peppermint tea or hot apple cider as a nightcap option so that the caffeine-averse aren't stuck with just water. Likewise, if you have "energy" mocktails (maybe you muddled some fresh ginger or used green tea in a punch), just make sure there's also a mellow option. Clearly label which drinks are caffeine-free on your bar signs so folks know. It can be as simple as writing "(decaf)" or "caffeine-free" next to the title.

- **Allergy Considerations:** This is less common in drinks than food, but still worth noting. If you use almond milk or any tree-nut product (orgeat almond syrup, for example, in a faux Mai Tai) or if you use something like seed-based flavorings (tonka bean, etc.), consider if any guests have allergies. When in doubt, let guests know: a small note on the recipe card like *"Allergy note: contains almond"* for the one drink that does, is very appreciated by those with allergies. Also, if you ever did a spicy mocktail with something unusual like chili or jalapeño, maybe label that too so spice-averse people aren't caught off guard. Most of the time, though, our mocktail ingredients are pretty gentle and all-inclusive.

BYO Alcohol – Yea or Nay? What if some guests *do* prefer a little booze in their drink? Since your event is zero-proof focused, you shouldn't feel obliged to provide alcohol. However, a gracious host can make an allowance if done tactfully. One approach: when inviting people or in your event notes, you can mention something like, *"We'll have an assortment of delicious alcohol-free cocktails. No need to BYOB – but if you'd like something stronger, you're welcome to bring a bottle for your own enjoyment."* This sets the expectation that alcohol isn't the star, but gives an open door for those who really want it.

In practice, you might have a few guests bring a bottle of wine or a flask. Handle it smoothly: have some wine glasses aside or a corkscrew handy, and let them pour their own. You don't have to integrate it into the main drink station (in fact, probably better if not, to keep the spirit of the zero-proof bar intact). They can spike their own cup discreetly. For example, I hosted a dry holiday party and one friend brought a bottle of rum – he ended up splashing a bit into the communal eggnog punch in his own cup. No one else really noticed or cared, because the punch was fabulous on its own. In another case, a partygoer arrived with a bottle of red wine for themselves; I simply gave them a glass and a quiet toast, and everyone was happy. Interestingly, when your zero-proof drinks are creative and tasty, most guests won't feel the need for alcohol at all. They might bring something "just in case" but then realize the mocktails are delightful and never open their bottle. Count that as a win!

If someone does ask, *"Hey, can I spike this?"*, you can reply cheerfully, *"Of course, feel free to add what you like to your glass – but do try it as is first, it's one of my favorite recipes!"* In fact, one Allrecipes user commented that at her party, she served a great fruity punch and *"for those who wanted some extra kick, I added champagne as I poured it into their cups. Yumm!"*. This way the base offering remained non-alc for everyone, but individual spiking was accommodated on the side. That's a perfect compromise.

The "Where's the Alcohol?" Question: You may get this classic query from a confused or cheeky guest. Be ready with a confident, positive answer. Own your alcohol-free theme with pride. For instance, say with a smile: *"Tonight, we're doing something different – all the fun, none of the alcohol. I've got a whole bar of zero-proof cocktails set up, you have to try the Sparkling Blood Orange Cooler, it's amazing!"* By immediately pointing them to the awesome alternatives on offer, you redirect the focus. Most people will go "Oh, cool!" and head off to explore the drinks. If someone presses, like "But really, why no alcohol?", you can keep it light: *"I wanted to create a unique experience – and give everyone a break from the usual. Trust me, your head will thank me tomorrow!"* said with a wink. Depending on your relationship, you can also mention reasons if you're comfortable (e.g. *"I've been experimenting with craft mocktails and I promise you won't miss the booze"* or *"We have friends coming who don't drink, so we thought let's make it great for everyone"*). Speak with the tone that this is intentional and fun – not something you feel you have to apologize for. When the host is enthusiastic and firm about the alcohol-free plan, guests typically relax and get on board.

Also, consider framing before the party even starts. If it's appropriate, let everyone know in advance it's a dry party, but in a way that builds excitement: *"Join us for a mocktail soirée – we'll have a create-your-own-cocktail bar (all delicious and alcohol-free)!"* When guests know what to expect, you reduce those questions altogether. Many might come curious about the cool mocktails you've hyped up.

Inclusive Activities (Focus on Fun, Not Alcohol): To ensure your gathering is memorable for its people and activities, plan things to do that don't revolve around drinking. If usually your friend group just stands around the bar at parties, you're going to change that dynamic – in a good way. Here are a few ideas to get folks laughing and bonding without a drop of alcohol:

- Party Games & Competitions: Never underestimate how a simple game can energize a party. It could be silly and active, like charades or Twister, or something strategic like a trivia quiz or card game. For mixed-age groups, games like Pictionary, Bingo, or a scavenger hunt can be hilarious. At a recent dry New Year's, we set up a "Minute to Win It" competition – short, goofy challenges (like who can stack the most marshmallows in a minute). The result: roaring laughter and zero attention on the nonexistent champagne. If it's a more intimate gathering, even a truth-or-dare Jenga (each Jenga block has a question or dare) can lead to fun revelations. Tailor to your crowd: the point is to get people interacting. When everyone is busy trying to beat each other at giant Jenga or solve a murder mystery game, they truly don't care what's in their glass.

- Music & Dancing: Create a space for dancing or karaoke. Sober karaoke is absolutely a thing – and sometimes even funnier because no one's slurring the lyrics. If you have a games console like Just Dance or a karaoke machine, set it up and watch people become stars after one or two mocktails. Live music works too; hire a local acoustic guitarist or have that friend who's great with a guitar perform a short set. Dancing is a natural high. As one wedding planner put it, *music and shared emotion can lift the celebration from pleasant to unforgettable–* no alcohol required. Plus, busting a move is a great way to break a sweat and get those endorphins going, which puts everyone in a great mood.

- Creative Stations: We mentioned photo booths and mocktail bars earlier. Think of other creative corners: maybe an arts & crafts station if it fits (decorate cookies, paint ornaments, make DIY party hats). At a Halloween party, you could have a *pumpkin carving or painting* contest – pair people up and let them go wild with designs (mind the sharp tools if kids are around!). For a baby shower, you might have a onesie-decorating station with fabric markers – again, something to do that isn't drinking. For game nights or movie nights, create a cozy "lounge" area with board games or a projector for a film – with plenty of popcorn and mocktail "movie drinks" like virgin pina colada smoothies. Interactive entertainment like a hired magician, caricature artist, or tarot card reader can also be awesome if budget allows – it gives folks an experience to talk about other than booze.

- Engage the Senses: One benefit of not having a booze-centric party is you can incorporate things that *wouldn't* mix well with heavy drinking. For example, you could do a short tasting session of something like gourmet chocolates, exotic fruits, or different international candies. People's palates are fresh and interested. Or set up a build-your-own sundae bar for dessert – sugar high, yes, but a joyful one. We did a "tea tasting" at one gathering – laid out 5 types of hot tea in air pots and little sample cups; guests actually enjoyed discussing the flavors (it was like a mini sober tea ceremony amid the party). These kinds of activities make the night feel rich and entertaining.

Above all, highlight the people and connections. Plan some moments that bring everyone together. Perhaps a toast (with mocktails) where you say a few words of gratitude or congratulations if it's an event like a shower or birthday. Or a group photo session when everyone's in goofy costumes or their ugliest holiday sweater – something that later when they look back at the pictures, they think about *how much fun they had with each other*, not the fact that no one was drinking. One dry event expert noted that including kids and families naturally shifts focus to "the simple joy of togetherness" instead of what's in the glass. If your gathering does include kids, embrace that: have kid-friendly games and let their energy infuse the adults. Without booze around, parents are usually less anxious and more willing to engage in kid-like fun too (yes, adults will enthusiastically join a piñata smashing or a hula hoop contest when sober!).

Finally, etiquette and attitude. Be prepared that one or two guests might take a light-hearted jab like "I could use a real drink!" – just laugh it off and say something like, *"Try the ginger-mint cooler first, it might change your mind!"* If someone is truly unhappy, well, that's on them – you've provided a wonderful spread. The vast majority will respect the vibe when they see how much effort and love you put into the alternative options. Lead with confidence: if you act like this is completely normal (which it is becoming, given the *sober-curious* trend), others will follow suit. Set the example by enjoying a mocktail yourself, initiating a fun game, and mingling. Your enthusiasm is contagious.

At the end of the day, hosting is about making memories. When your friends reminisce about your party, you want them to say, *"Remember how we all sang together by the piano?"*, or *"That was the night we invented that crazy mocktail with the cotton candy – and it actually tasted good!"*, or *"I met so-and-so at your party and we had such a great conversation over those fruit punches."* These are the markers of a successful celebration. If anyone laments, *"I don't even remember what happened, but I know I drank a lot,"* – well, that tends to be the after-story of a booze-heavy night, not one of yours. By planning an inclusive, activity-rich, zero-proof event, you ensure everyone leaves with memories of the people, the laughter, the flavors, and the fun, rather than a hazy recollection centered on alcohol. And that, host, is the ultimate win for hospitality.

In summary, zero-proof celebrations truly are for *any* time of year and *every* kind of guest. You now have tips to adapt recipes seasonally, deck out your space with creative themes, streamline your serving process, and welcome each guest with thoughtfulness. As you mix and mingle through all of life's events – from holidays to ordinary days made special – you'll prove that festive spirit doesn't come from a bottle. It comes from the company we keep, the care we put into the details, and the joy of raising a glass (of something delicious and alcohol-free) together. Happy hosting, and cheers to many memorable, zero-proof gatherings ahead!

Chapter 7

New Traditions, Lasting Memories – Embracing Zero-Proof Celebrations

The holidays are a time of warmth, connection, and celebration. In this chapter, we'll explore how zero-proof gatherings – festivities without alcohol – are creating new traditions and lasting memories. Embracing alcohol-free hosting isn't just a trend; it's a meaningful lifestyle choice that prioritizes wellness and inclusivity. As you read on, you'll discover the many benefits of zero-proof celebrations and see how you, as a host, are part of a positive cultural shift towards more mindful and healthy festivities.

Wellness-Focused Celebrations

Choosing to host alcohol-free celebrations can enrich your life and the lives of your loved ones. Imagine waking up the morning after a holiday party with no next-day regrets – no pounding headache or hangover, just a clear head and happy memories. That's a key benefit of zero-proof gatherings: you get to enjoy every moment of the celebration and still feel great the next day. In practical terms, *saying goodbye to hangovers* means the nausea, headaches, and tiredness that often follow a night of drinking are replaced by an improved mood and fresh energy. Instead of needing a day to recover, you and your guests can stay productive and upbeat.

Another major perk is better sleep. While a nightcap is often thought to help one relax, alcohol actually disrupts your sleep cycle and prevents deep, restful sleep. By skipping the booze, you're more likely to get a full night of rejuvenating slumber. Many people find that when they celebrate without alcohol, they fall asleep more easily and wake up feeling truly rested. Along with better sleep comes staying hydrated and energized throughout the party. Alcohol is a diuretic – it dehydrates the body, which can leave you feeling sluggish. In contrast, zero-proof drinks keep you hydrated, so you maintain steady energy and even notice benefits like brighter skin and a clearer complexion (since alcohol can dry out the skin). In short, an alcohol-free holiday bash lets you have all the fun without the physical downsides.

These health and wellness advantages aren't just personal anecdotes – they're part of why *zero-proof gatherings are a rising trend*. More hosts and party-goers are embracing the idea that you don't need alcohol to have a festive atmosphere. In fact, the movement toward alcohol-free celebrations aligns with a broader cultural shift toward mindful consumption and self-care. People are increasingly aware of how alcohol impacts their health, and many are choosing to moderate or forego drinking in order to feel better. Surveys show growing participation in initiatives like "Dry January" and the "sober curious" movement, indicating that skipping alcohol is becoming mainstream. This mindful mindset is visible in younger generations especially. For example, Gen Z (today's young adults) drinks about 20% less alcohol than Millennials did at the same age, focusing more on wellness and mental clarity. They've helped drive demand for sophisticated alcohol-free alternatives and have shown that socializing doesn't have to revolve around booze.

All of these factors have contributed to an explosion in the non-alcoholic beverage market. What was once a niche idea is now a booming industry. According to market research from The Freedonia Group, retail sales of non-alcoholic alternatives (from zero-proof beers and wines to spirit-free cocktails) are projected to grow at an average rate of 18.5% annually through 2029. That is extraordinarily high growth, driven by shifts in consumer behavior and emerging wellness trends. It signals that booze-free fun is *here to stay*. Far from being a temporary fad, alcohol-free celebrating is becoming a lasting part of our culture. When you choose to host a wellness-focused, zero-proof celebration, you're not just taking good care of your guests – you're joining a positive change in how we all socialize and celebrate. You can feel good knowing that your party is as healthy as it is joyful, and that you're on the cutting edge of a movement that prioritizes good times *and* good health.

The Gift of Inclusive Hosting

Think of zero-proof entertaining as a gift you give to your guests – and to yourself as the host. By choosing to make your holiday gathering alcohol-free, you're creating an environment where everyone feels considered, comfortable, and welcome. There's a special kind of hospitality in offering drinks and festivities that *all* guests can enjoy, regardless of age, drink preference, or dietary needs. No one has to feel awkward about declining a drink or worry that there are no festive options for them. The designated driver can join in the toast with a delicious mocktail in hand. Friends who are pregnant, avoiding alcohol for health reasons, or who simply don't like to drink will feel fully included rather than singled out. Inclusive hosting means every guest – from the cocktail lovers to the teetotalers – has something fun and flavorful in their glass and can partake equally in the celebration.

By hosting inclusive zero-proof gatherings, you send a message of care and respect. You're saying, "I've thought of everyone, and I want each person here to have a fantastic time." This approach often puts guests at ease and encourages more meaningful connections. Without alcohol as a social crutch, people tend to engage more in conversation, games, or activities, leading to genuine memories together. And as the host, you get to stay fully present to orchestrate the fun, all while knowing you won't have any mishaps or regrets to manage. In many ways, hosting without alcohol can reduce social pressures; guests don't feel obliged to drink to fit in, and that creates a relaxed atmosphere where the focus is on the *people* and the *occasion* rather than the beverages.

Zero-proof entertaining has such broad appeal now that it's even becoming a trend in gift-giving and home bartending. High-quality alcohol-free cocktail recipe books and premium zero-proof drink mixers are hot items on the market. In fact, alcohol-free cocktail guides have become sought-after gifts in their own right. For example, a popular sober lifestyle publication's 2024 holiday gift guide showcased "12 Alcohol-Free Recipe Books & Non-Alcoholic Brands" – a curated list of zero-proof recipe books and drink products for people who want to have fun with sophisticated booze-free options. This kind of gift guide (featured on The Sober Curator website) highlights how mainstream and desirable alcohol-free entertaining has become. Not long ago, a book of mocktail recipes might have been considered niche, but now it's a thoughtful present for the wellness enthusiast or home entertainer in your life. Perhaps you've received such a gift yourself, or maybe you're using this very book, *Zero-Proof Celebrations*, to plan your own parties. Either way, by valuing inclusive, alcohol-free hospitality, you're tapping into a new kind of celebratory spirit – one that appreciates creativity and flavor without the liquor.

Consider also that when you host a zero-proof party, you might be inspiring others. Your friends and family could be pleasantly surprised by how fun and flavorful an alcohol-free gathering can be, and they may carry that inspiration into their own events. Some might even ask for your drink recipes or party planning tips. In this way, every zero-proof celebration you host is a gift that keeps on giving: it spreads the idea that celebrating *everyone* is possible and delightful. Whether you're using this guide to throw an unforgettable holiday party or gifting it to a friend who loves to host, you are helping to normalize and spread inclusive hosting. You're showing that festive drinks don't require booze to be special. The more people experience this, the more the movement grows. It's a virtuous cycle – by treating your guests to an inclusive, zero-proof bash, you encourage more hosts to do the same, and together you all contribute to a cultural shift where no one has to feel left out. That truly is a gift worth giving.

Looking Ahead – Mindful Drinking's Future

What might holiday celebrations look like in five or ten years? If current trends are any indication, the future is bright (and bubbly – with *sparkling cider*, that is!). It's easy to imagine a New Year's Eve in the near future where mocktail bars are just as common and crowded as champagne bars. Perhaps you'll stroll through your city's holiday market and find pop-up booths selling artisanal alcohol-free punches and hot mulled mocktails alongside the usual fare. On New Year's Eve, half the crowd might be clinking glasses of alcohol-free sparkling wine at midnight, proving that everyone can ring in the New Year in style, whether or not they drink alcohol. This optimistic picture isn't so far-fetched – even today there's a wave of sober bars opening across the U.S. (places like Hekate in New York City, Sans Bar in Austin, and The Sober Social in Atlanta) to accommodate changing attitudes about alcohol. Five years from now, seeing a chic zero-proof cocktail bar on every main street could be the new normal.

In workplaces too, mindful drinking is set to become standard. Office holiday parties, which once revolved around spiked eggnog and open bars, are already evolving. It's increasingly common for companies to include craft zero-proof drinks by default, ensuring that company celebrations are both fun *and* responsible. We can foresee a time when every corporate gathering has an alcohol-free drinks table as well-stocked as the alcoholic one – if not more so. Imagine an office party where the signature drink of the night is a rosemary pomegranate spritz (with no alcohol), and nobody has to worry about overindulging in front of colleagues or how to get home safely. This inclusion will make work events more comfortable for everyone, catering to all employees' choices. The overall trend is that mindful drinking – the practice of being intentional about alcohol consumption, or choosing not to drink – will weave itself into all sorts of festivities, from family feasts to community events. In the future, having plenty of zero-proof options will be as expected as having vegetarian options on a dinner menu: simply a given.

Behind these changes are not only consumer preferences but also big shifts in the beverage industry. Major beverage companies and trend analysts are predicting continued expansion and innovation in the zero-proof market. The business world has noticed that more people are moderating their drinking or abstaining entirely, and they're responding with a flood of new products for this growing audience. Global sales of no- and low-alcohol drinks are surging year over year. In the U.S. alone, *no-alcohol* beverage volume grew about 20% in 2023 and is forecasted to keep climbing sharply – one report projects a +17% compound annual growth rate from 2023 to 2028 for the non-alcoholic category. Similarly, an international study by IWSR (a leading drinks market analysis firm) expects the no-alcohol segment to expand by about 7% volume CAGR through 2028, adding billions of dollars in value. For context, those growth rates are strikingly high compared to most food and drink categories. What it means is that companies are investing in creating ever more flavors and innovations for alcohol-free drinks. We're already seeing a blossoming of creativity: zero-proof spirits that taste like gin or whiskey, but are made from botanicals without the booze; craft near-beers that closely mimic IPAs or stouts; ready-to-drink mocktails in a can with gourmet ingredients. Each year, the flavors get more convincing and the offerings more diverse, from adaptogenic relaxer drinks with herbs and teas, to sophisticated sparkling aperitifs. The future promises even more exciting alcohol-free choices on store shelves and bar menus.

Crucially, the cultural acceptance of not drinking is growing fast, led largely by younger generations. We've talked about Gen Z's influence – their comfort with not drinking has helped destigmatize the choice to stay sober or drink lightly. Millennials too are driving the no-alcohol market: one analysis found that Millennials make up a majority of non-alcoholic beverage consumers, enthusiastically trying new zero-proof products and even alternating them with regular drinks as part of a balanced lifestyle. This means the social narrative is changing. It's becoming perfectly acceptable (even cool) to be the person at the party with a mocktail in hand, or to host a gathering without serving any alcohol. The more common this becomes, the more celebrations center on connection, experience, and authenticity rather than on intoxication. People are realizing that the real "spirit" of the holidays comes from the laughter, the conversations, the music and dancing, the traditions we share – none of which actually require alcoholic spirits at all.

A modern "dry bar" serving creative zero-proof cocktails – scenes like this are becoming part of mainstream holiday nightlife. As we look ahead, it's clear that mindful drinking is not a passing fad but a lasting evolution in how we celebrate. Trend analysts are confident that zero-proof options will keep expanding, and even traditional alcohol brands are launching alcohol-free versions to keep up with demand. We can expect more bars and restaurants to feature dedicated alcohol-free sections on their menus, if not entire venues that are booze-free. It's very possible that New Year's Eve in a few years will have as many people cheers-ing with alcohol-free bubbly as with champagne. And when you throw a party, you might find guests asking eagerly about your mocktail recipes because that's the highlight of the night for them. By being an early adopter of the zero-proof party trend, you're ahead of the curve. You're a trendsetter in your circle, showing others what festive, healthy entertainment looks like. In a world that's shifting toward wellness and inclusivity, you're leading by example – and having a blast doing so. The future of holiday gatherings is heading in a direction where everyone can participate fully, and you're already making that future a reality today.

A Final Toast to Change

As we conclude our journey through festive, alcohol-free hosting, let's raise one last imaginary glass together. Fill it with your favorite zero-proof drink – be it a spiced cranberry spritzer, a frothy hot cocoa, or a zingy ginger-mint mocktail – and join in a toast to all the joyful, inclusive gatherings to come. Cheers to good times and good health – the spirit is in the celebration, not in the spirits! Through each chapter, we've seen that memorable holidays don't need alcohol at all; what they need is heart, creativity, and care for the people around us. By stepping into your role as a mindful host, you've shown that you have all of that in abundance.

This final toast is a *celebration of you* as much as it is of the zero-proof movement. You've embraced a hosting style that prioritizes wellness and welcome. You've learned how to craft delicious drinks that everyone can enjoy, how to set a mood that doesn't rely on a cocktail shaker's rhythm, and how to start new traditions that leave no one out. You are proving that the holidays can be full of warmth, laughter, and connection – all while leaving your guests clear-headed and truly cared for. Your commitment to inclusive entertaining means that every clink of glasses at your table is a moment of genuine camaraderie. And the memories made at your gatherings? They'll be vivid and joyous, unmarred by anything except perhaps the natural giddiness of the season.

As you go forth to create your own zero-proof traditions, feel confident and excited. You're joining countless others in redefining what celebration means. No matter the occasion – Thanksgiving, Christmas, Hanukkah, New Year's, birthdays, or just a Saturday get-together – you now have the tools and inspiration to make it special without alcohol. When you host your next party, you can do so knowing that you're giving people an experience that's fun *and* healthy. The next morning, everyone will have fond memories and zero headaches, and that is truly something to celebrate.

So here's to you, the mindful host who is helping shape a new era of celebrations. With each toast you lead and each alcohol-free drink you serve, you're proving that the real spirit of the holidays lives in our connections and kindness. These are new traditions you're building – ones based on inclusion, wellness, and authenticity – and they are sure to bring lasting memories for years to come. Cheers to change, to traditions made fresh, and to a holiday spirit that shines brighter than ever! Enjoy every moment of your zero-proof celebrations, knowing that you're making the season special in a way that leaves everyone smiling.

Epilogue

As you close this book and prepare for your next gathering, remember that the most memorable celebrations have never depended on what fills the glasses—they've always been built on the warmth of connection, the joy of shared laughter, and the thoughtfulness of a host who truly cares.

Throughout these pages, we've explored how alcohol-free entertaining opens doors to inclusive experiences that welcome everyone at your table. You've discovered that mocktails can be just as sophisticated as their spirited counterparts, that seasonal ingredients create magic in unexpected ways, and that the art of hospitality transcends any single element of your menu.

The recipes you've learned will serve you well, but the principles behind them will serve you even better. Thoughtful preparation, attention to detail, and genuine enthusiasm for bringing people together—these are the ingredients that transform ordinary moments into extraordinary memories.

Your guests will remember the fizzing pomegranate sparklers that caught the light just right, the warming spiced ciders that chased away winter's chill, and the elaborate garnish stations that became conversation starters. More importantly, they'll remember feeling truly included, genuinely celebrated, and completely at ease in your home.

The holiday traditions you create today will ripple forward through generations. Children who grow up seeing celebration and sophistication without alcohol will carry those values into their own homes. Friends who discover they can have just as much fun at your alcohol-free gatherings will begin hosting their own.

Each time you choose to celebrate without alcohol, you're making a statement that joy doesn't require justification, that festivity comes from the heart, and that the best parties happen when everyone feels welcome.

Your next celebration awaits—and now you have everything you need to make it unforgettable.